modern

asian flavors A Taste of Shanghai

Richard Wong
founder of chinablue

photographs by Noel Barnhurst

CHRONICLE BOOKS
SAN FRANCISCO

Library of Congress
Cataloging-in-Publication
Data available.
ISBN 10: 0-8118-5110-9
ISBN 13: 978-0-8118-5110-7

Manufactured in China.
Designed by Jana Anderson,
studio A design.
Food and prop styling by Sandra Cook.
Photographer's Assistants:
Noriko Akiyama, Sara Johnson Loehmann,
Gene Lee, June-Young Lim.
Food Stylist's Assistants:
Elisabet der Nederlanden, Penny Zweidinger.

Distributed in Canada by
Raincoast Books
9050 Shaughnessy Street
Vancouver, British Columbia
V6P 6E5

10 9 8 7 6 5 4 3 2 1

Chronicle Books LLC
85 Second Street
San Francisco, California 94105
www.chroniclebooks.com

*Buderim Ginger is a registered trademark of
Buderim Ginger Limited. Chinablue is a
registered trademark of Chinablue Inc. Sears
is a registered trademark of Sears, Roebuck and Co.*

acknowledgments

For eight years, I have read *The Polar Express* to Ursula and Christina every holiday season, yet when I saw the movie and the face of the boy at the moment he heard the bell ring—that moment he believed in Christmas—it became one of those memories I will always cherish and embrace. In my lifetime, that scene captured the essence of who I am, what I am, and why I am.

For those who heard chinablue's bell ring, I truly wish to express my most heartfelt thanks. Because of each and every one of you believing in me, I am writing this today.

I would like to acknowledge first two special women: Rosemary Brooks for encouraging me to share my life story, and Leslie Jonath for embracing the idea of a Shanghai family in America. They were my guiding stars.

To Kristen Sager, the maestro of this book, and Pat Hagerty, for patiently testing each recipe. A warm hug.

To Sally Geller, Jean Armstrong, Chris Bridge, Sandy Kortright, Jan Weaver Marshall, and Renee Benke for your dedication to my vision. Your loyalty is a breath of fresh air.

To Deborah Chae, Jane and Chris Cook, Christine and Joe Montz, Cindy and Mark Kishel, Janet and Tom Fall, Rita and Creighton Jenkins, Cynthia Weinmann, Christina and John Fay, Christina Laskowski, Shirley Richie, Art Montz, John Bell, John Bell Jr., Bill Ziegler, Maria and Eric Clothier, and Miranda and Orlando Lobo for just believing. Thank you.

To Pat Pearson, Anne Paxton, and Steve Carnavale, when life appeared insurmountable, they showered me with grace.

To Penni Wisner, whom I can call a friend and a fabulous writer. You brought the heart and soul of this book to life.

To Jana Anderson and Pamela Geismar, to whom I gave my trust and name in creating this beautifully designed book. You two were the Yin to my Yang.

And to my mother, May, and my mother-in-law, Nancy, for their devotion to me. I love you both.

When you believe, each moment is a joy, every day is wonderful, and time is everlasting. Do you hear the bell ringing?

This book is dedicated to my wife, Susan, and our beautiful daughters, Ursula Marie and Christina May, who, I hope, will think wonderful thoughts of their dad's life.

In memory of my father for his love of life. He is my inspiration.

table of contents

preface

My family lived in Shanghai for perhaps ten or twelve generations. Then we fled, arriving in the United States in the mid-1960s. We did not talk much about the past.

But my mother, who did not know how to cook when she arrived here, remembered the taste of her native dishes. She set about recreating those particular flavors. Every day, she fed my father, my brother, and me the same foods she and my father had grown up enjoying. Without saying a word, she taught me about my past. Through food, she gave me my heritage and kept the memory alive.

Today, I have a wife and two daughters. And I cook my family's recipes for them. We visit my mother, my aunts, and my grandmother. In each home, we rediscover more of our cultural history through shared meals.

Those flavors and the example set by my mother, my father, and my grandparents continue to inspire me every day. Family recipes, in fact, are the basis of the sauces, oils, and dressings produced by my company, chinablue. Through it and this book, I invite you to join the feast.

introduction

Even when I was very young, just two or three years old, I loved the local Shanghai crabs. We ate them warm from the steaming kettle with a cold dipping sauce. My mother says she still remembers her surprise that I would sit at the table, working on my crab, peeling away the shell, and picking out the sweet meat.

Shanghai hairy crabs have always been a seasonal delicacy, to be enjoyed in the autumn. But this was the early 1960s, during the Cultural Revolution, and our family was not allowed to have crab. We got them, as we did the milk my brother and I drank, from the black market. One night my grandfather called to say he had gotten hold of some crabs and we should come right over; his cook was about to drop them into the cooking pot. My parents bundled us up and took us to grandfather's house to enjoy the impromptu, clandestine feast.

Shanghai in those days was just a shadow of itself relative to its heyday of the early twentieth century. The British sailed into Shanghai in the early 1840s. Soon, the small trading port located on China's central coast close to the mouth of the Yangtze River transformed itself into a center of international commerce. Everyone—Chinese, Europeans, Americans, Japanese, Russians, Indians—came to Shanghai to get rich. Everything in the world was for sale in the shops and it was the hub of trade in distinctly Chinese goods, too: tea, silk, and yes, opium.

Shanghai—"Pearl of the Orient" and "Paris of the East"—became a cosmopolitan city of wealth, elegance, optimism, and energy. The multinational population influenced the city's cuisine. Restaurants of every sort abounded and chefs strove to outdo each other and borrowed techniques and ingredients to incorporate into their cooking. Shanghainese cooking became a natural fusion cuisine.

In the 1990s, the Chinese government allowed the socialist market economy to reassert itself in Shanghai. With its characteristic drive to excel, the city set about recreating a twenty-first-century version of its former self. With a population of more than fourteen million, Shanghai is the largest city in China. The Shanghai Stock Exchange, when completed, will be the world's tallest building and a powerful symbol of the reemergence of Shanghai as it lays claim to its old title of Paris of the East.

Shortly after that crab dinner, however, my family fled China. We went first to Hong Kong and, after several years, received visas for the United States. My father, a college graduate, returned to school to earn an American degree and worked throughout his schooling. My mother, who had never been allowed in the kitchen while in China except to instruct the cooks, now had to learn to cook. Her sister, who had arrived in the States in the 1950s, assisted her since, by the time we arrived, she had become a very good cook. And I needed to become a real American, not a Chinese-American. An American. It was very important then to become a citizen. I have vivid memories of standing beside my father in 1969 at the Toledo, Ohio, courthouse as he laid his hand on his heart and became an American citizen.

I grew up in the Midwest in the '60s and '70s eating only authentic Shanghainese cooking. Every day, I went home from school for lunch. So I know it is possible to cook this kind of food without easy access to a Chinatown! And I know that the flavors appeal to just about everyone. My fraternity brothers in college taught me this.

Like many college kids, I did not like the food provided, so I thought I would cook some of my mother's specialties. I burned everything. After that, my aunt sent me care packages. All I had to do was boil noodles and reheat her prepared ingredients and I had dinner. And so, to my chagrin, did my friends.

I didn't try cooking again until I moved to California in the early 1980s to pursue my career in architecture. I went to dinner at the house of a Shanghainese woman I had met at a family wedding. When I tasted her food, I was stunned. The dishes she cooked had the same flavors I had grown up with. We looked back over our family histories and discovered we were related five different ways. Because we shared relatives, we also shared family recipes. By Chinese standards, we were family. That experience taught me that the flavors our family imbued into even classic Chinese and Shanghainese dishes were identifiable and unique. They were unlike anything available in local restaurants.

I decided to learn more about my heritage by cooking our family recipes. My girlfriend at that time, who was also from Shanghai, and I spent hours cooking every night. Then I would ask for specifics from my mother, my aunts, and my grandmother. My grandmother's cooking was both rich and intense, a flavor profile I strive for in my own cooking. Often when I visited her, she would send me home with a big jar of a Chinese version of spaghetti sauce (see page 125). If I went off on a business trip, I could count on my roommates to have polished it off by the time I got back. They didn't think of it as Chinese food, just delicious food.

Within a few years, my friends would come over for dinner before we all went out. Shanghainese Slow-cooked Chicken (page 73) was a particular favorite. It would take me several hours to prepare. So one day I decided I would buy a really big pot and make a very large batch of the sauce to save time. And everyone went home with a jarful. They wanted to have the same flavors they enjoyed at my house but without the work.

I never thought of having a food company until I started asking my friends what they did with those jars of sauce. I asked one young woman if she had made my recipe. "Oh, no," she replied, "I barbecued chicken, and my family loved it." Despite her reassurances, I was sure it would not taste good. Then I tried it myself. She was right. I asked other friends how they used the sauce. They used it when they grilled, baked, and sautéed. They drizzled it on vegetables or even over rice. For me, each sauce was simply a shortcut to recreate a single dish. But my friends applied my sauces in ways I would not have imagined, for instance, smearing Tangy Ginger Sauce (page 30) on salmon and grilling it. Or cooking sesame-soy with chopped mushrooms to make an Asian-flavored tapenade (see page 51).

My company, chinablue, began in 2000 with four sauces. They were the sauces for my four favorite dishes, but by then my friends had convinced me that the flavors were universally appealing and just as widely applicable to any cooking style. I began to believe that I could show the world something about the elegance and sophistication of Shanghainese culture through food.

Many of the recipes contained in this book are my family's recipes, handed down from one generation to the next. They are what I call modern dishes. Modern in the sense that the recipes are timeless—they were recognized as excellent a hundred years ago and taste great today. A good example is the Slow-simmered Star Anise Duck (page 78).

You also will find recipes that my friends taught me as they experimented with chinablue sauces and added them to their favorite recipes and cooking methods. These I call "cross-over" dishes. The Skewered Sesame Chicken (page 74) and the Black Bean–Grilled Flank Steak (page 89) are two examples. When you taste those dishes, you may find it difficult to identify them as Chinese. Instead, they simply taste delicious.

A common misperception people have of Chinese food is that it is always stir-fried and served hot. But many Shanghainese dishes and many in this book are served at room temperature. I think most of my food tastes better the longer it sits. It is ideal food for entertaining because so much of it can be done ahead.

My purpose with my company, chinablue, and with this book is to demystify Asian cooking and to provide authentic Chinese flavor combinations that you can apply to your way of cooking. Even while we developed and tested recipes for this book, we kept thinking of new ideas for salad dressings, marinades, cocktails, and entrées not classically Chinese, such as rabbit, leg of lamb, and veal shanks. I hope that the recipes provide an introduction to and inspiration for adding Asian flavors to your daily cooking.

the shanghai-style pantry

I think cooking should be fun and simple. Especially Chinese cooking. Many people I meet assume they need a long list of exotic ingredients. But, for our first day of test cooking, I did all the shopping in twenty minutes at a single—very good—grocery store.

I went to Chinatown for just three ingredients: pickled snow cabbage, seasoned tofu, and dried Chinese noodles. Then I discovered that these three ingredients or close substitutes were available in a large San Francisco supermarket.

Chinese typically shop daily and insist on high quality and freshness. If you decide to go to a Chinatown, it's true that the shopkeepers speak various dialects of Chinese and some of the ingredients will look entirely unknown. But there are markets that are more accessible than others. You just have to find them. Many cooking schools and other organizations give walking tours of Chinatowns. Or ask among your friends. Maybe one of them already knows where to go, or knows someone else who does. It can feel like taking a vacation to an exotic place, but you are only discovering something new about your own city.

To prepare the material for this chapter, I spent a good deal of time in the Asian ingredient aisle of a large supermarket. Even for me, the array looked bewildering. Stir-fry sauces, teriyaki sauces, chili oils, and chili sauces. Seemingly hundreds of soy sauces. How can anyone make sense of all this?

First, focus. You need very few ingredients to cook the dishes in this book. Second, the label's ingredient list is your best friend. Ingredients relate directly to flavor. For instance, the less water, the more flavor. Look for familiar ingredients. Two products labeled "satay sauce" may have very different ingredient lists. Don't assume a sauce looks red because it contains chili oil or sauce; it might be food coloring. Caramel coloring can sometimes be added to soy sauce.

A nice, syrupy body may be the result of corn syrup, because it's far less expensive than cane sugar. When you taste a product and read its ingredient list, you understand why it is often necessary to pay more.

You can divide and conquer by categorizing products into five flavors: savory, sweet, spicy, tangy, and pungent. Savory sauces are usually based on soy, the primary ingredient in almost all Asian cooking. An example would be sesame-soy, a sauce used for a classic Shanghainese slow-cooked dish with chicken (see page 73); it's also delicious as a sauce for noodles, as a marinade, and as a wok sauce.

Sweet sauces are also often based on soy. Teriyaki and all its variations fall into this category. Chili provides the base for spicy sauces, while vinegar and/or citrus offset with sugar create tangy sauces like the Tangy Ginger Sauce (page 30). Sauces like oyster sauce, based on fermented oysters and ingredients such as dried shrimp, impart a pungent flavor. While a few of my recipes do use dried shrimp, I do not often cook with oyster sauce, and so have not discussed it here.

Shanghainese generally do not cook with garlic. But if you like it, choose a product that includes it. As with all food and cooking, let your preferences tailor your choices.

ingredients

Chinese pastes, condiments, and sauces were developed as a way to give an inexpensive bulk food—rice—taste. Because Chinese sauces are so versatile, once your pantry is stocked, you can instantly create quick, flavorful meals. Use sweet soy with citrus juice and zest for vinaigrette. Add black bean sauce for savory grilled or sautéed fish or red pepper sauce for fire. Need a snack quickly? Dried Chinese noodles cook in three minutes. Then layer on flavor the way my father did: Drizzle the noodles with soy sauce and sesame oil, then add a dab of Chinese sesame seed paste, and finally a good splash of Shanghainese Red Pepper Sauce or Spicy Chili Bean Sauce (page 34). If you have carrots or cucumber, you can shred and add them, too.

Black bean sauce: The main ingredients should be salted (also called fermented) black beans and soy sauce. Some will include garlic. If the ingredients include chilies, you are actually looking at a *hot bean paste*. When using the sauce as a marinade, do not thin it but spread it onto the ingredient, or massage it in. When cooked, the sauce will loosen.

Chili oil: There is a difference between spicy and hot. Spicy is about flavor and heat is about intensity. The point with chili oil is heat. Ingredients should include hot chilies and oil, and sometimes garlic or sesame oil. Mixed with soy sauce, chili oil is most commonly used as a dip. On its own, I like to pour it over noodles. I also use it to add heat and color to a finished dish such as Hot and Sour Soup (page 59) and as an ingredient in, for example, a peanut sauce.

Chili sauce: This is a bright red blend of hot chilies, salt, vinegar, and sometimes garlic and sugar. You might think of it as a very hot ketchup. And lots of people do use it that way, but I prefer to use it as an ingredient, as in the Shanghainese Red Pepper Sauce and the Spicy Chili Bean Sauce (page 34). The chili *bean sauces* you see on store shelves include primarily one or more types of fermented beans, such as black beans, soybean paste, broad bean paste, and chilies. They are not as hot as hot bean pastes but are rich, full, and spicy in flavor. Chili *paste* differs from chili sauce. If a chili sauce is like a fresh tomato sauce, chili paste is like tomato paste. For the paste, the chilies are salted and fermented. The flavor and texture is far more concentrated than in chili sauce.

Chinese dried salted black beans: These are soybeans that have been salted and fermented. They have a wonderful savory flavor delicate enough to be teamed with crab, shrimp, and scallops as well as meat and vegetables. They come in a plastic bag. Once opened, transfer the beans to a clean jar and refrigerate. Because the beans can seem dirty, I usually recommend rinsing them very quickly before use, and then chopping or mincing them. Do not confuse salted black beans with canned soybeans or dried black beans (turtle beans). Neither will substitute for salted black beans.

Cooking oil: In my cooking, I work to remove water from foods to concentrate flavor. Oil is my ally because oil carries and intensifies flavor. Shanghainese cooking uses a good deal of oil, so choose a good-quality oil with a neutral flavor at a comfortable price. During testing, we used safflower, corn, soybean, and vegetable oils and they all worked well. I like an organic soybean oil I have recently discovered in a health food store. Until now, my preferred cooking oil has been a refined sesame oil (see more about sesame oil below), but it's expensive.

Dried Chinese black mushrooms: They are also called shiitake mushrooms and can be found in the Asian ingredient aisle of the supermarket. Make sure to keep them in a tightly closed container or they may attract bugs. You can, of course, use fresh but the flavor and texture are different from those of the dried.

Dried Chinese noodles: This style of noodle is made of wheat flour, water, and salt. We Chinese do cook our noodles al dente, but to us it means "slightly chewy." The noodles can be found in the ethnic section of many supermarkets. Packages labeled "Chinese" noodles or "Chinese-style" noodles are very thin, round noodles. We also use a flat noodle; for this style, you are most likely to find packages labeled Japanese udon noodles. You can substitute angel hair pasta or vermicelli (also called cellophane noodles, made from mung beans). I cook the noodles in boiling, salted water with a splash of vegetable oil added to prevent them from sticking to each other. I often give them a quick rinse in hot water, then drain again. Fresh Chinese noodles usually include egg. Sometimes you can find fresh wheat noodles, and, if the noodle maker comes from Shanghai, you may be lucky enough to find the thick, round noodle called Shanghai noodles that we love to put in soups.

Dried shrimp: You will need to look for these in Chinatown or in markets that specialize in ethnic ingredients. They come in many sizes because they are used in various ways; for instance, in some dishes they are added whole. Shrimp labeled "extra large" may be just the size of your thumbnail. The shrimp do have a distinctive flavor, but they are not as pungent as many would fear. I enjoy the slightly chewy texture and burst of flavor that whole shrimp add to a dish, but it is perfectly fine to mince them. Soak them in dry sherry before use. Sometimes I add a few dried shrimp to a pot of rice while it cooks to add flavor.

Dry sherry: This is an absolute staple for me. My mother uses sherry as well as Shaoxing, a rice wine from close to Shanghai, adding a drop, for instance, to chicken soup just before serving. But I have found that its flavor is too particular for most of the people I cook for so I limit myself to a pale, dry, cocktail sherry.

Ginger: Ginger is one of my favorite flavors and a primary ingredient in Chinese cooking. Many recipes begin by sautéing ginger and scallions in oil. Sometimes you can find baby ginger in Chinatown and in specialty markets. Nearly white because it has not yet developed its characteristic brown skin, it is more delicate in aroma and flavor than mature ginger and has few, if any, fibers. It does not need to be peeled. Keep a large knob of fresh, mature ginger in your refrigerator's vegetable drawer. Peel and chop it just before use.

Ginger juice is particularly useful to have on hand for making drinks. Bottled ginger juice is available or you can make your own ginger juice by wrapping minced ginger in cheesecloth and squeezing it over a bowl. Recently, I discovered that prepared minced ginger is available in grocery stores. It is all flavor and no fiber!

Peanut sauce: Many of these dot store shelves, so it is very important to read ingredient labels in order to know what you are buying. Peanut is not even always the first ingredient. Since there is always peanut butter at my house, I make my own. That way I can adjust the heat and spice to my liking.

Peppercorns, white and black: Use freshly ground pepper. I use white pepper for presentation—if the food is light colored, for instance, white fish or noodles, then I use white pepper.

Red pepper flakes: I prefer to use red pepper flakes (also called chili flakes) rather than ground red pepper such as cayenne because the flakes add greater visual interest and texture to foods. Plus, I think flakes have a longer shelf life than ground.

Salt: Soy sauce often provides all the salt flavor a dish needs. But sometimes color matters. For example, in a rice salad or fried rice, I like to maintain the whiteness of the rice and the clear, contrasting colors of the other ingredients, so I add salt. To add soy would turn everything brown.

Sesame seed paste: None of the recipes in this book call for sesame seed paste, but it has always been a favorite flavor. Unlike tahini, Chinese sesame seed paste is made from toasted seeds and is dark in color. Combine it with soy sauce, ginger, chilies, sherry, vinegar, and honey or sugar and you have an incredible sauce for hot or cool noodles and even potatoes or yams. Peanut butter makes a good substitute.

Sesame-soy sauce: This is such a basic—and delicious—flavoring for Asian food that several versions of this savory sauce can be found on supermarket and specialty store shelves. It can be used as a marinade, wok sauce, and as a dressing for noodles or rice. But to realize its full potential—for chinablue's version, at any rate—slow cook with it (see page 73). The primary ingredients are as the name implies: sesame oil and soy sauce. But other versions might include various additional ingredients, such as sesame seeds, citrus flavoring, ginger, sherry, vinegar, and so on.

Smoked country ham, such as Smithfield: People may be surprised by our liberal use of ham and the prevalence of pork in our menus. But China has an ancient tradition of preserving, including pickling and salt curing. Every year, my mother buys a whole Smithfield ham. The Chinatown butchers cut it into thick, three-inch slices that my mother passes out to the family. We keep it on hand in the refrigerator to use as needed for dishes such as Not-fried Rice (page 115). The Smithfield hams are the closest to the smoked hams in Shanghai.

Soy sauce: I grew up on Japanese (Kikkoman) soy sauce, not because my mother could not get Chinese soy sauce, but because our family prefers the taste of Kikkoman. It's a well-made, consistent, all-purpose soy sauce appropriate for all types of cooking, sauces, and dips. Lite soy sauces have less salt and a less complex flavor than regular soy sauce. Low-salt soy sauce should be used as a finishing sauce—for sushi or as a dip—and not as an ingredient. It would be like cooking with skim milk instead of whole milk. Chinese dark soy sauce includes molasses so that it can better coat pork ribs.

Star anise: Star anise shares a flavor profile (licorice) and the essential oil anethole with aniseed, but it is not botanically related. Star anise has a fine, delicate aroma, especially when only the pods are used instead of both seeds and pods. It's a classic pairing with pork and poultry and it is one of the five ingredients in Chinese five-spice seasoning, a sweet, hot, aromatic blend of star anise, fennel seed, cinnamon, cloves, and Szechuan pepper. The number five is powerful, as it reflects the Chinese belief in the five elements: earth, metal, wood, fire, and water.

Toasted sesame oil: Along with soy sauce, this is a primary ingredient in Chinese cooking. It can also be called dark sesame oil. Most is made from toasted white sesame seeds from which the oil is extracted. (This is why it can sometimes taste burnt. Return any bottle to the store that tastes like that.) Buy an unblended 100 percent sesame oil. Once opened, a bottle keeps about eighteen months in a cool, dark pantry. Toasted sesame oil is a finishing oil; do not cook with it. Instead, take your dish off the heat and add a splash of oil. The heat will release the oil's aroma. Refined sesame oil is clear and almost neutral in flavor.

Tofu: Tofu originated in China, where it occupies a place held by dairy products in the West. The tofu-making process releases the essential amino acid lysine that rice lacks. When rice and tofu are combined in a dish or meal, all the building blocks of a complete protein are then available. We Shanghainese enjoy tofu in all its forms—some of which may be unknown to most Westerners—such as bean curd sheets, sold in flat bundles or rolled into long sausages. These can have almost a meaty flavor and are used to make vegetarian pressed duck. We love silken tofu for its smooth, flan-like texture and the way it absorbs flavor. We also like pressed, seasoned tofu, dicing it and adding it to cold and hot dishes alike. You can find this in many markets, where it is called "baked" tofu. It comes in a vast array of flavors. The closest to a Chinese seasoned tofu would be one flavored with Chinese five-spice, or look for one labeled "soy." Any time a seasoned tofu is called for in the following recipes, you can always substitute plain, firm tofu.

shanghainese sauces

At our house, we were rarely just family at table but were often joined by other Shanghainese families or relatives. Every meal was a celebration, not just of family, but of food. Many dishes would be served at once, family style. There would be a dish each of chicken, pork, fish, and vegetables. The foods would provide contrasts in taste—from savory to spicy—color, and texture. Always there would be rice. In addition, there would be many small dishes of condiments, including salted peanuts, diced pickled radish, hot sauce, and soy sauce.

When my mother would cook for a formal party, she would start several days in advance. Many Chinese dishes, especially Shanghai-style ones, can be made ahead, improve in flavor as they sit, and are served at room temperature.

Each sauce in this chapter is based on an original recipe for a Shanghainese dish as cooked by my family for generations. Each was born as a stand-alone recipe as a way to save time in the kitchen. The flavors, like Shanghainese cuisine generally, are rich, complex, and mildly spicy. The secret ingredient of much Shanghainese cooking is sugar. A little sugar balances the heat of chili and smooths and tames the intensity of soy sauce. The sugar gives the whole dish a fuller, deeper flavor.

Add a little oil and Tangy Ginger Sauce (page 30) can be a salad dressing. Add some sparkling water and you have a refreshing spritzer. Yet the sauce is a traditional dipping sauce for steamed crab. Its sweet/tart flavor exemplifies classical Shanghai cooking. But if you taste it as a dessert sauce (see page 130), you won't recognize it as Chinese, only as really delicious. The same idea holds true, I believe, for all the recipes in this book.

Each of the sauce recipes takes only a few minutes to make. Most of the ingredients probably already exist in your kitchen: salt, sugar, sherry, soy sauce, vinegar, and sesame oil. Tasting and cooking with the sauces will give you an immediate experience of authentic Shanghai flavors. You will also be better able to judge other similar sauces and marinades.

After making them at least once as they appear here to establish a reference point, feel free to add garlic if you like—Shanghainese do not cook with garlic—and vary other ingredient proportions as well. Please note, too, that these sauces will provide all the flavoring for a dish; you generally will not need to add any other seasonings, such as salt and pepper. You can double and triple the sauce recipes as needed for the dishes in this book.

tangy ginger sauce

½ cup apple cider vinegar

7 tablespoons sugar

1 teaspoon soy sauce

¼ cup very finely minced peeled fresh ginger

This is a variation on our family's dipping sauce for steamed, fresh crab. Its clean, tart-and-sweet flavor enhances the crab's sweet meatiness. It is one of the first sauces I created for my company, chinablue. Tangy Ginger Sauce is great as a dressing for greens or fruit salads, to pour over vegetables, or to marinate salmon, or as a sauce for steamed, grilled, or baked fish. The sauce gives flavor to simple stir-fry dishes when added for the last few minutes of cooking. The flavor is a great inspiration for desserts as well. The recipe may be doubled.

Heat the vinegar, sugar, and soy sauce together in a small pan just until the sugar has melted. Pour the mixture into a bowl, add the ginger, stir well, and refrigerate until cold. The sauce will keep, tightly covered, for several days in the refrigerator.

Makes about 1 cup

sweet scallion sauce

⅓ cup vegetable oil

½ bunch scallions, white and green parts, very finely sliced (about 1 cup; see Note)

6 tablespoons sugar

1 tablespoon plus 1½ teaspoons salt

1 tablespoon very finely minced peeled fresh ginger (optional)

1 teaspoon finely grated lemon zest (optional)

Freshly ground white pepper (optional)

This is from my mother's recipe for fava beans (see page 109), one of my very favorite dishes. It is a terrific marinade and basting sauce for pork and chicken. If you prefer zesty flavors, add the optional ingredients listed. Remember that this sauce will provide all the seasoning needed for a dish so you will not need to add any other, such as more salt. Certainly you can make this ahead of time, but I think the flavor is best when made the same day. The recipe can be doubled.

Heat the oil in a small sauté pan over medium-low heat. Add the scallions and mix well. Add the sugar, salt, and, if using, the ginger, lemon zest, and a pinch of white pepper. Stir well again. Cook very slowly, stirring often, to dissolve the sugar and cook the scallions, 5 to 10 minutes.

Makes about 1 cup

Note: Scallions (green onions) are the yin to ginger's yang. I use them a great deal, stir-fried with ginger to form a base flavor for a dish and scattered on top of dishes as a colorful and crisp garnish. They are delicious on their own, grilled and drizzled with sweet soy sauce. Use every part, white and green, discarding only the roots and dried out green tips.

Variation for Spicy Scallion Sauce: Use 3 parts Sweet Scallion Sauce to 1 part Spicy Chili Bean Sauce (page 34); that is, add ⅓ cup Spicy Chili Bean Sauce to the above recipe. If you like spicy flavors, add more Spicy Chili Bean Sauce to taste, up to 2 parts Sweet Scallion to 1 part Spicy Chili Bean Sauce.

shanghainese red pepper sauce

2 teaspoons cornstarch

6 tablespoons soy sauce

½ cup sugar

¼ cup dry sherry

2 tablespoons chili sauce or chili sauce with garlic (see page 20)

2 packed tablespoons very finely minced peeled fresh ginger

2 teaspoons toasted sesame oil

This spicy and hot sauce was the flavoring for a dish of chicken and bell peppers that my mother would make. She would use ginger slices, and then discard the ginger before serving. But I like the bite of ginger, so I mince it and leave it in the sauce. Any time you want to add spice and heat to a dish, reach for your Shanghainese Red Pepper Sauce. Use it for marinating meat, fish, and poultry, as a wok sauce, to pour over noodles, and even as a dip or table sauce. You may well want to double the recipe to make sure you have enough on hand.

Stir the cornstarch together with a tablespoon of the soy sauce in a small bowl and set aside. Measure the remaining soy sauce, sugar, sherry, chili sauce, ginger, and oil into a small pan and bring to a boil over medium heat. Stir the cornstarch mixture again, and then stir it into the pan. Simmer gently for about 1 minute, and remove from the heat. Pour the sauce into a bowl or jar and let it cool before use. Store, tightly covered in the refrigerator, for up to 1 week.

Makes about 1 cup

Variation for Spicy Chili Bean Sauce: (Used mostly for seafood or simply over rice or noodles.) Add 3 tablespoons minced salted black beans (see page 21) to the Shanghainese Red Pepper Sauce and stir well to break up any clumps of beans.

sweet soy sauce

2 teaspoons cornstarch

½ cup soy sauce

6 tablespoons sugar

2 tablespoons dry sherry

This is a variation of my grandmother's basting sauce for pork ribs. A sweet, soy-based sauce is a common ingredient in Asian cooking, especially in China. Japan's version is teriyaki. Once upon a time, teriyaki was made by boiling soy sauce and sake together until they became a syrupy, intense sauce. This sauce simplifies that long preparation process. The result is an incredibly versatile sauce with a velvety texture. Mix it with a little orange juice and zest plus a splash of lemon for a salad dressing. Or drizzle it over freshly steamed vegetables. Brush it on fish, chicken, or pork, whether sautéing, grilling, or steaming, and use it as a wok sauce. Or mix it with molasses for an incredibly rich, glossy marinade and glaze for meatballs (see page 46). The only problem with sweet soy is that you may find yourself eating it by the spoonful! The recipe may be increased or decreased as needed.

Stir the cornstarch together with a tablespoon of the soy sauce in a small bowl and set aside. Measure the remaining soy sauce, sugar, and sherry into a small pan over medium heat. Stir until the sugar dissolves. Stir the cornstarch mixture again, and then quickly add it to the pan. Stir and cook gently for about 1 minute, and then pour the sauce into a bowl and chill until needed. Store, tightly covered in the refrigerator, for up to 1 week.

Makes about ⅔ cup

star anise sauce

4 teaspoons cornstarch

⅔ cup soy sauce

½ cup vegetable oil

½ cup dry sherry

½ cup sugar

5 large star anise pods

This is my shortcut version of a sauce for cooking duck. Star anise is indigenous to China and plays a prominent role in Shanghainese cuisine. The aromatic cinnamon and sweet licorice notes of the spice make it a natural flavor combination with duck and pork. Typically, it is used for slow cooking, for example, for Slow-simmered Star Anise Duck (page 78). But you can pour a little into soups and stocks to give them an intriguing aroma. Because of its smooth, slightly syrupy body, Star Anise Sauce makes a great wok sauce for any quickly cooked dish including pork, chicken, duck, or turkey. The recipe may be proportionately increased or decreased.

Stir the cornstarch together with two tablespoons of the soy sauce in a small bowl and set aside. Measure the remaining soy sauce, oil, sherry, sugar, and star anise into a small pan over medium heat. Bring to a gentle simmer and cook for about 1 minute. Stir the cornstarch mixture again, and then add it to the pan. Stir and let the mixture simmer for another minute. Remove the pan from the heat and let cool. Do not discard the star anise, but leave them in the sauce. Pour the sauce into a bowl or clean jar with a lid and set aside until needed. Store, tightly covered, in the refrigerator for up to 1 week.

Makes about 1⅔ cups

asian salad dressing

This dressing is actually my mother's recipe for pickling juice. But I have found it to be a very versatile salad dressing. Its light, tangy taste with a hint of spiciness makes it especially suitable for cabbage salads. But I use it for lots more: I splash it on noodle and rice salads and use it on raw or cooked spinach or chard. Its flavor balance allows it to meld flavors that might otherwise seem too strong, for instance, in one of my favorite salads, a mixed green salad with blue cheese and cranberries (see page 62).

½ cup apple cider vinegar (see Note)

¼ cup sugar

Salt

1 teaspoon toasted sesame oil

Freshly ground white pepper

Red pepper flakes

Whisk the vinegar, sugar, and a large pinch of salt together in a small bowl until the sugar has dissolved. Add the oil and season the dressing with a good pinch of white pepper and another good pinch of red pepper flakes. Whisk vigorously, then taste and adjust the seasoning. If you do not use all the dressing, store in a clean glass jar with a nonreactive lid in the refrigerator for 1 week or more.

Makes about ⅔ cup

Note: Shanghainese use apple cider vinegar as their vinegar of choice rather than distilled white vinegar or rice wine vinegar, the common choices in most other parts of China.

cocktails and appetizers

blood orange-tini

Our team at chinablue, especially Rosemary Brooks, loves the beautiful red color the blood orange juice gives to this drink. And we love the combination of citrus and ginger juice, too. With this drink, let me make the first toast: Welcome to our world of Shanghai style. Cheers!

Crushed ice

Juice of 1 blood orange

1½ tablespoons ginger juice
(see page 22)

1 tablespoon honey tangerine juice

3 ounces high-quality vodka or gin

2 long strips of blood orange zest

Fill a cocktail shaker ⅓ full with crushed ice. Add the blood orange juice, ginger juice, honey tangerine juice, and vodka. Close the shaker and shake vigorously until the contents are very cold. Strain into 2 chilled martini glasses and drop an orange twist into each.

Makes 2 drinks

ginger-tini

6 small pieces crystallized ginger

8 large ice cubes

4 ounces lemon-flavored vodka

2 tablespoons ginger syrup
(see Note) or 2 tablespoons sugar
dissolved in 2 tablespoons ginger
juice (see page 22)

2 very thin lemon slices

My father made great martinis. On the weekend, after their tennis doubles matches, my father's friends would come over for rounds of martinis. Ginger is a terrifically cooling flavor in the summer. This version of a martini is guaranteed to perk up appetites on a hot night.

Place 3 pieces of crystallized ginger in each of 2 chilled martini glasses.

Fill a cocktail shaker with the ice, and then pour in the vodka and ginger syrup. Shake well and strain the drinks into the prepared glasses. Float a lemon slice on top of each cocktail.

Makes 2 drinks

Note: I use a ginger mixer from the Australian ginger specialist Buderim called Ginger Refresher. It is a ginger syrup meant to be used as a mixer with soda water, for instance.

lychee-tini

One 20-ounce can lychees

8 large ice cubes

6 ounces lemon-flavored vodka

Too often, lychees are reserved for dessert at a Chinese restaurant. You receive several dull white fruits in a plain bowl. But make them the basis for a martini, and you have something exciting. The drink tastes, well, sexy. It has that indescribable tropical aroma—bath powder, marshmallows, vanilla, and fruit. Perhaps that doesn't sound like something you would necessarily drink, but try it and I think you will more than like it.

Strain the juice from the lychees and reserve the fruit and juice separately. You should have about 1¼ cups juice. Place 2 lychees in each of 4 chilled martini glasses and set aside the remaining fruit for another use. Fill a cocktail shaker with the ice. Add the lychee juice and vodka. Shake well. Strain the drinks into the prepared glasses.

Makes 4 drinks

Note: Any leftover fruit makes a great "cook's snack," to be nibbled while cooking. Or skewer each fruit with a toothpick, arrange in a bowl, and serve with the drinks. You might also make them into a smoothie by pureeing them with other tropical fruits.

shanghainese iced tea

1 cup boiling water

10 balls black pearl green tea or other green tea

6 ounces bourbon

4 ounces Cointreau or orange-flavored liqueur

2 ounces freshly squeezed orange juice

4 ice cubes

4 thin orange slices (optional)

Black pearl tea is a very fragrant green tea from China. The long leaves are hand rolled into tight balls that open and slowly release their flavor and aroma as the tea steeps. Both men and women drink wine and hard spirits in Shanghai, though they traditionally would not do so in each other's company. Shanghainese men seem to love scotch and bourbon, drunk in a short glass with a single ice cube. I've used ten balls of tea per cup of water here, not only because the tea is powerfully scented, but because ten is a number of completion. And this would be a great drink to enjoy after completing a day of work or a tennis match.

To brew the tea: Pour the water over the tea in a teapot or bowl, let it cool to room temperature, and then chill.

For each drink: Pour ¼ cup cold tea into a short tumbler or cocktail glass. Make sure to have 1 or 2 balls of tea in each glass. Add 1½ ounces bourbon, 1 ounce Cointreau, and ½ ounce orange juice to the glass. Stir, add 1 ice cube, and fix an orange slice onto the rim of the glass, if desired. Repeat for the remaining 3 drinks.

Makes 4 drinks

spicy grilled chicken wings

1 pound chicken wings

½ cup Shanghainese Red Pepper Sauce (page 34)

Vegetable oil for brushing grill pan

In China, the colors of food are symbolic. Yellow means wealth and prosperity, while red symbolizes blood and life. My mother and now I, too, cook by color. She will frequently say while a dish cooks, "It is not red enough," and then add more sauce to give the color she wants. We have learned to judge the intensity of flavor by the intensity of the color. This is why I baste almost constantly while I grill. The color and the flavor build by layers as the cooking progresses. You can also make this dish with Sweet Soy Sauce (page 35) and Sweet Scallion Sauce (page 33) to vary the flavor.

Disjoint the wings into 3 pieces each, save the tips for stock, and put the rest in a medium bowl. Pour the sauce over the chicken pieces and toss well. Let the chicken marinate for at least 10 minutes and preferably 2 hours in the refrigerator.

Preheat a grill to medium-high heat. Brush a wire rack or pan with oil. Grill the chicken, basting continuously with the marinade. Turn the pieces occasionally, and grill until they are cooked through, about 15 minutes, depending on the heat of the grill. Serve immediately.

Serves 4

Note: I use my nonstick grill pan almost every day. Then I can grill, rain or shine, any season of the year. It is particularly handy since I can pop an underdone ingredient right back over the heat. Also, after grilling a steak, for instance, I will sometimes slice it and return it to the grill pan. I pour over any remaining marinade and turn the meat in the marinade until it is very reduced and the meat is glazed.

shanghainese mini-meatballs

1 pound ground pork

1½ cup Sweet Soy Sauce
(page 35), divided

2 tablespoons molasses, divided

½ cup vegetable oil

These are my grandmother's meatballs. Sometimes she would turn them into a stuffing for a sort of dumpling. She had a large ladle she would partially immerse in hot water and then pour in a little egg. By swirling the ladle, she would create a sort of egg pancake. She popped a meatball into the ladle and folded the egg pancake over it to create a half moon. I can eat about thirty of those all by myself. Food like that lets you know you are loved. Chinese dark soy sauce includes molasses. The molasses helps the sauce stick to meats such as ribs and adds a rich flavor, too. Here, it helps glaze the meatballs. The sauce is a lustrous, almost black color like liquid chocolate. You will use part of the soy sauce and molasses to prepare the marinade, ideally 1 day in advance.

In a medium bowl, mix together well the meat, 1 cup of the sauce, and 1 tablespoon of the molasses. Cover and refrigerate the mixture overnight (see Note).

Form the meat by tablespoonfuls into small balls. Heat the oil in a flat-bottomed wok or large sauté pan over high heat. Cook the meatballs, a few at a time, shaking the pan and keeping them moving so they do not stick, until they are crusty all over, about 5 minutes.

Take the pan off the heat, and return all the meatballs to the pan. Add the remaining ½ cup sauce and 1 tablespoon molasses, and toss to coat the meat well. Reduce the heat to medium, cover the pan, and bring to a simmer. Cook for about another 5 minutes at a gentle simmer. Uncover and swirl the pan, moving the meatballs in the simmering sauce so the sauce glazes the meatballs. Keep swirling the pan, coating the meatballs in sauce until the sauce is very reduced and syrupy. Turn the meatballs out into a deep serving platter or bowl and serve.

Serves 4

Note: The overnight marination allows the meat to absorb all the sauce so, when shaped, the meatballs do not break apart during cooking. If you do not have time to chill the meat overnight or to mix it in the morning to make in the evening, you can knead about 1 cup dried bread crumbs into the meat to hold it together during cooking. Made without binders such as bread crumbs, the meatballs are incredibly juicy.

star anise cups

This is a simplified version of a classic Chinese recipe, minced squab in lettuce cups. The slight bitterness of crisp endive provides a nice counterpoint to the sweet, rich flavor of the dish. Feel free to substitute butter lettuce and even iceberg. If you do use iceberg, be sure to trim the leaves into round, bowl shapes. When served in larger leaves, this makes a terrific first course or luncheon dish.

⅓ cup vegetable oil

1 pound ground turkey thighs

½ to ¾ cup Star Anise Sauce (page 36)

2 large cucumbers (about 2 pounds), peeled, seeded, and cut into ⅛-inch dice

1 cup salted pistachios, coarsely chopped

2 heads endive, leaves separated

Heat the oil in a flat-bottomed wok or sauté pan over medium-high heat and add the turkey. Stir with a wooden spoon to break the meat into small bits. A splatter guard is helpful here.

As the meat begins to release its juices, add about ¼ cup of the sauce and stir. Reduce the heat to maintain a rapid simmer and continue to cook, stirring well, until the liquids are very reduced. Add another ¼ cup of the sauce and continue to simmer rapidly, occasionally stirring and tossing the meat until it is dark brown and rich looking. Taste and add the remaining sauce, if desired, and simmer another few minutes. Remove the mixture from the heat and let it cool for about 10 minutes to allow the meat to absorb the cooking liquids.

Toss the cucumbers and nuts together in a medium bowl and then add the meat and any liquids left in the pan. Mix well until all the ingredients take on a nice sheen. Fill each endive leaf with a heaping tablespoon of the mixture and arrange the leaves on a platter.

Serves 6 to 8

tea eggs

Tea eggs are traditionally served on the Chinese New Year. The egg symbolizes birth and prosperity. They are served whole and unpeeled so that everyone opens their own treasure. The longer the eggs sit in the liquid, the darker they become and the more flavorful.

12 eggs, hard boiled

1 cup soy sauce

4 teaspoons salt

12 star anise pods

12 black tea bags

Gently crack the shells of the eggs all over by tapping them with the back of a spoon but do not remove the shells. Put them in a large nonreactive saucepan with the soy sauce, salt, star anise, and enough water to just cover the eggs, about 8 cups. Tie the tea bags together and place them in the pan with the eggs.

Bring to a boil over high heat. Reduce the heat and simmer gently, covered, about 12 minutes. Turn off the heat and set the pan aside. Let cool to room temperature, covered. Refrigerate the eggs overnight in their cooking mixture before serving.

Serves 8 to 12

mushroom tapenade

My dear friend Stephanie Rach taught me to make this dish. It's easy to make ahead of time and terrific to have on hand. Use any type of mushrooms or combination you like, such as cremini, button, and mini portobellos. Serve it with crackers and crusty bread as an appetizer or as a dip with carrots, celery, and colorful strips of bell pepper, toss it with noodles for supper, or serve it as a side dish to chicken or pork.

⅓ cup vegetable oil

12 ounces assorted fresh mushrooms, finely chopped

⅔ cup sesame-soy sauce (see page 24)

Crackers or sliced French bread for serving

Heat the oil in a flat-bottomed wok or a large sauté pan over high heat. Add the mushrooms and stir well. Add the sauce and bring to a boil.

Cook, stirring frequently with a wooden spoon, until the pan is nearly dry and the mushrooms are thoroughly cooked, dark, and glossy, about 10 minutes. Scrape the mushrooms into a serving bowl and serve them with crackers or French bread.

Makes about 1½ cups; serves 6 to 8

Note: A gadget always in use at my house is a splatter guard, a circle of stainless steel mesh with a long handle. Much of the cooking I do involves rapid simmering and sautéing or stir-frying. These can create a mess on the stove top. That in itself can be enough to dissuade some cooks from trying a recipe. So the splatter guard can be a cook's best friend—no mess around the pan, no spots on your shirt.

tangy ginger crab

1 live Dungeness crab
(about 2 pounds)

About ½ cup Tangy Ginger Sauce
(page 30), chilled

Simple food. Sweet, warm crab and tangy, cold sauce. Even as a little boy in Shanghai, I loved to eat local crab. But the only ones we could get were from the black market. You can buy a cooked crab for this dish, but my experience of precooked crabs is that they are often watery and flavorless. It's no more difficult to cook a live crab than it is to boil pasta—boil some water, and pop in the crab. And the taste is amazing, sweet, and meaty.

In a large steamer, bring several cups of water to a boil. Place the crab in the steamer, cover, and steam until the crab has turned bright red and is cooked through, about 15 minutes. Remove the crab and let rest until cool enough to handle.

Insert your thumb or a knife point between the upper shell and the body, opposite the mouth. Pry off the shell, and then trim off the mouth and other inedible parts. Scrape the yellow-green liver (tomalley) out of the center of the body.

Leaving the legs attached, cut the crab in half, down the middle, with a large knife. Then, cut each half into thirds so each piece has legs and body. Crack each section of leg by giving it a good whack with the knife. Be careful not to cut all the way through.

Serve the crab on a platter with a small bowl of very cold Tangy Ginger Sauce.

Serves 2 to 3

soups and salads

grandmother's chicken soup

1 whole chicken (about 4 pounds)

1 large bunch scallions

3 ounces fat from a smoked country ham such as Smithfield, cut into several pieces

1 large knob (about 1 ounce) fresh ginger, sliced

Sugar (optional)

About ¼ cup dry sherry, plus more as needed

1 bundle fresh bean curd sheets (about 2 ounces), cut into 1-inch squares

Salt

4 large handfuls (about 4 ounces) fresh spinach

2 ounces smoked country ham such as Smithfield, shaved into 8 thin slices

My grandfather insisted on a three-course meal for lunch and dinner every day of the week. It took my grandmother twenty years to rebel. He then compromised, declaring that a soup served at lunch could reappear at dinner. For this soup, each bowl should have a big piece of the ham floating on top. Good Chinese manners require that everyone admire the ham, praising it for its size and depth of color. Country hams are expensive—a big piece means the host recognizes the value of the guest. Ham is not just a garnish; it's the secret ingredient in the soup, giving it a unique savory taste. Serve the soup with chopsticks. Sip the soup from the glass or bowl and pick out the solids with chopsticks. Seaweed and bean curd sheets are a traditional garnish, or Chinese noodles, water chestnuts, and pea shoots would also make good additions to the soup.

Rinse and clean the chicken. Inside the cavity, run your thumb deep along both sides of the base of the tail to remove the bloody tissue there. Rinse again.

Choose a deep pot or stockpot that fits the chicken snugly. Add water to cover the chicken, and then add the scallions, ham fat, ginger, and sugar, if using. Add the neck, heart, and gizzard of the chicken, if desired, but not the liver. Place the pot over high heat, cover, and bring to a boil.

Reduce the heat to maintain a lively simmer and cook, covered, about 1 hour. Add the sherry and continue to simmer rapidly, with the lid on, until the broth is very fragrant, about 1 hour more.

continued

Strain the broth into a bowl and cool. Set the chicken aside until cool enough to handle, then pull off and reserve the meat. Discard the bones, skin, scallions, and ginger. When the fat has come to the surface of the broth, spoon it off and discard, or reserve it for dishes such as Sautéed Sweet Pea Shoots (page 114). Or refrigerate the broth until the fat congeals, and then lift it off.

To serve, return the broth to a large pot and bring to a gentle simmer over medium heat. Add the chicken meat and bean curd. Add salt to taste and, if desired, add a few tablespoons of sherry just before serving to add extra aroma and flavor.

For a pretty presentation, use glass bowls or heavy, clear glass tumblers. Put a handful of spinach leaves in each and ladle in the broth. Make sure each portion receives some chicken and bean curd, and garnish it with a piece of the ham.

Serves 8

Note: Chinese would serve the heart and gizzard as snacks. We tend not to eat the liver since it is the blood's filtration system. It would also discolor the broth.

hot and sour soup

This is a traditional Chinese chicken soup. It would open a meal for a Chinese but could make a meal for many Americans. Feel free to add more or less of any of the ingredients, plus any others you might like. I used bamboo shoots here because they are traditional but they can easily be omitted. To keep the color of the soup clear, I keep the soy sauce to a minimum and adjust the seasoning with salt. If you use homemade stock with good body, you will not need to use cornstarch.

3 cups homemade chicken stock or low-salt canned chicken broth

7 ounces firm tofu, cut into matchstick-size pieces

¾ cup bamboo shoot strips (see Note)

4 ounces pork, cut into thin lengths

1 ounce dried Chinese black mushrooms (see page 21), rehydrated and finely sliced

2 tablespoons soy sauce

1½ tablespoons seasoned rice vinegar, rice vinegar, or distilled white vinegar

1 tablespoon dry sherry

1 teaspoon sesame oil

1 teaspoon cornstarch (see recipe introduction)

Salt

¼ teaspoon freshly ground white pepper

Chili oil for serving (see page 20)

Sliced scallions for garnishing

Put the stock in a large saucepan and bring to a simmer over medium heat. Add the tofu, bamboo shoots, pork, and mushrooms and simmer for about 5 minutes.

In a small bowl, mix together the soy sauce, vinegar, sherry, sesame oil, and cornstarch (if using) and mix well. Stir the soy mixture into the soup and simmer gently another few minutes. Taste and adjust the seasoning with salt and white pepper.

To serve, divide the soup among 4 bowls and drizzle a little chili oil over each. Scatter scallions over the surface and serve immediately.

Serves 4

Note: Bamboo shoots are a traditional, crunchy Chinese ingredient. They are canned whole, sliced, or cut into strips. You will find the most choice—and the largest—cans in Chinatown. On super-market shelves, you will most likely find small, 8-ounce cans of sliced bamboo shoots, yielding 5 ounces after draining, enough for this recipe.

cherry tomato and cucumber salad

Chinese cooks seek balance in every aspect of a dish, not just in flavor, but also in color, texture, even presentation. In this salad, sugar balances vinegar, crisp balances tender, and the red and green of the tomatoes and cucumber skin look vibrant against the white cucumber flesh.

1 English cucumber
(about 1 pound), thinly sliced

1 pint basket cherry tomatoes

¼ cup Asian Salad Dressing
(page 37)

If the cucumber seems watery, press the slices between sheets of paper towel or in a tea towel. Then, arrange the cucumber slices with the cherry tomatoes in a deep platter or bowl. Pour the dressing over the mixture, and let it sit for about 5 minutes before serving.

Serves 4

Note: I prefer English or hot-house cucumbers because they are firmer and less watery. You don't need to peel or seed them unless you prefer to for presentation purposes. If I am using regular cucumbers, I peel them, split them in half lengthwise, and scrape out the seeds with the tip of a spoon. To dice the cucumber, cut each half into even slices, lengthwise. Then cut these crosswise into even dice.

seasonal mixed green salad

We Chinese prefer our vegetables cooked rather than raw as salads. But my friends have broadened my palate. Here, the Asian flavors of the dressing balance the Western pungent flavors of blue cheese and the sweet snap of cranberries.

6 ounces mixed baby salad greens

3 tablespoons (plus more if desired) Asian Salad Dressing (page 37)

½ cup dried cranberries

Generous ¼ cup crumbled blue cheese

In a salad bowl, toss the greens with the dressing. Taste and adjust the amount of dressing, if desired. Add the cranberries and blue cheese and toss gently. Serve immediately.

Serves 4

asian cole slaw

In Shanghai, we use cider vinegar, while the Cantonese use white vinegar. Use different colors of bell peppers to make a confetti slaw of white, green, yellow, red, and orange. I have never been able to shred cabbage as finely as you find in Chinese restaurants, so I was delighted to discover packages of very finely shredded "angel hair" cabbage at the local supermarket. This slaw would taste great piled on top of grilled hamburgers made from meat mixed with a healthy dose of Shanghainese Red Pepper Sauce (page 34).

One 12-ounce package (about 7 cups) angel hair or finely shredded cabbage

2 cups shredded carrots

1 large red bell pepper, very finely julienned

½ to ¾ cup Asian Salad Dressing (page 37)

In a large bowl, toss together very well the cabbage, carrots, and bell pepper with ½ cup of the dressing. Let stand for about 10 minutes. Taste, and adjust with more dressing, if needed. Chill well before serving.

Serves 4 to 6

chinese chicken salad

In this version of Chinese chicken salad, the peanuts are gone, replaced with a savory soy and sesame flavor heightened by a gingery tang. I find many versions of Chinese chicken salad to be aggressively crunchy. This one soothes—the lettuce wilts slightly when tossed with the hot noodles.

Ginger Salad Dressing

2 tablespoons toasted sesame oil

¼ cup soy sauce

3 tablespoons apple cider vinegar

2 tablespoons sugar

2 teaspoons finely minced peeled fresh ginger

1 large skinless, boneless chicken breast (about 9 ounces)

Salt

2 tablespoons vegetable oil, divided

4 ounces flat, dried, Chinese noodles (see page 21)

2 teaspoons toasted sesame oil, divided

5 ounces mixed salad greens

To make the ginger dressing: Whisk the sesame oil in a small bowl with the soy sauce, vinegar, sugar, and ginger. Mix well until the sugar has dissolved.

Put the chicken and half the dressing in a bowl or large plastic bag. Coat the chicken well and set aside for about 20 minutes or overnight in the refrigerator.

Bring a large pot of water to a boil, add a large pinch of salt and 1 tablespoon of the vegetable oil. Add the noodles and cook until they are still chewy, about 5 minutes. Do not rinse, so that the starch remains on the noodles. Drain and pour into a bowl or platter and toss with 1 teaspoon of the sesame oil.

Heat a grill pan coated with the remaining 1 tablespoon vegetable oil over high heat. Add the chicken and baste frequently with the marinade as the chicken cooks. Cook until just cooked through, turning once, about 8 minutes, depending on the thickness of the breast.

While the chicken is cooking, combine the greens with the noodles and the remaining dressing. Toss gently; the greens should wilt slightly in the warmth of the noodles. Arrange them on a serving platter.

Remove the chicken to a cutting board and slice it thinly across the grain. Return it to the hot pan, pour any remaining marinade over it, and, working quickly so the chicken does not overcook, turn the slices over in the marinade until glazed. Arrange the chicken on top of the salad and drizzle it with the remaining 1 teaspoon sesame oil. Serve at room temperature.

Serves 4

poultry and meat

lemon chicken

This is my friend Lenora Yih's recipe. She lived in Hong Kong and learned it there from her family's Cantonese cooks. They make the sauce with chicken stock, bridging the flavors of the sauce and the fried chicken. Her recipe is Shanghai style and emphasizes flavor contrasts. The lemon sauce omits stock and gets flavor from honey and lots of fresh lemons. Made right, lemon chicken is incredibly delicious—crunchy, crispy, and never oily. You can pour the lemon sauce over the chicken or serve it on the side as a dipping sauce.

Lemon Sauce

1 teaspoon cornstarch

⅓ cup freshly squeezed lemon juice

¼ cup sugar

2 tablespoons honey

Salt

1 Meyer or Eureka lemon, cut into very thin rounds (optional)

1 large egg

2 teaspoons salt, divided

⅓ cup tempura batter mix (see Note)

¼ teaspoon freshly ground white pepper

1 pound skinless, boneless chicken breasts, cut into 1-inch cubes

About 3 cups vegetable oil

To make the lemon sauce: Stir the cornstarch together with a little of the lemon juice in a small bowl and set aside. Measure the remaining lemon juice, sugar, honey, and a pinch of salt into a small saucepan and bring to a boil over medium heat. Stir the cornstarch again, and then add it to the pan. Stir well and simmer gently for 1 minute. Take off the heat and set aside.

Arrange the lemon rounds around the edge of a deep serving plate or bowl, if desired. Set aside until needed.

Crack the egg into a shallow bowl and whisk in ¼ teaspoon of the salt. In a medium bowl, whisk together the tempura batter mix, remaining 1¾ teaspoons salt, and white pepper.

Dip each piece of chicken first into the egg and then into the tempura batter mix. Turn to coat the pieces well and remove them to a plate or rack. Set aside until ready to cook.

Pour the oil into a medium flat-bottomed wok or sauté pan to a depth of at least 1 inch. Place over high heat and heat until the oil smokes. Add the chicken pieces carefully to the hot oil. Regulate the heat to maintain the temperature at 350 to 375° F. Stir and turn the chicken pieces until they are golden and crisp all over, about 5 minutes. Remove to a plate lined with paper towels.

Reheat the lemon sauce over low heat until it barely comes to a boil. Put the chicken on the prepared serving platter or bowl and pour the sauce over it or serve the sauce in separate bowls as a dipping sauce.

Serves 4

Note: You can find tempura batter on the Asian ingredient aisle of most supermarkets.

Note: My favorite sauté pans are actually flat-bottomed woks. They heat fast and their wooden handles stay cool. They are also light, very easy to maneuver, and can be purchased with a nonstick coating. With a little practice, you will soon find yourself swirling and tossing ingredients like a pro. It is not necessary, however, to buy new pans. Cook any of these recipes with your favorite skillet or sauté pan.

spicy stuffed bell peppers

1½ pounds ground turkey thighs

3 ounces button mushrooms, finely chopped

1 large egg

1¼ cups Shanghainese Red Pepper Sauce (page 34)

6 large bell peppers

¼ cup vegetable oil

The amazing thing about this recipe is that you do close to nothing—the peppers cook on low heat and need only an occasional stir—and the dish ends up with an incredibly intense, rich flavor. When my mother made these, she used only green bell peppers and stuffed them with ground pork. Hers were savory, but I added spice to my version and lightened the recipe by using ground turkey thighs. Depending on your timing, marinating the meat can vary from thirty minutes to twenty-four hours. A longer marination allows the flavor to penetrate the turkey, mellowing the spice flavor. Using peppers of uniform size but different colors makes a pretty presentation.

In a large bowl, mix together well the turkey, mushrooms, and egg. Stir in the sauce and set aside to marinate for at least 30 minutes.

Cut around the stems of the peppers and lift out the cores. Use your fingers to loosen the seeds and pull out the ribs. You want to leave the shoulders of the peppers intact to hold in the filling. Fill each pepper completely with the turkey mixture, packing it tightly. Set aside whatever filling you do not use.

Pour the oil into a large, deep saucepan or sauté pan in which the peppers fit comfortably in a single layer. Place the peppers carefully in the pan with the bottoms up (stem sides down). Spoon any remaining filling around the peppers. Cover, place the pan over low heat, and bring to a gentle simmer.

continued

After 20 minutes, check that the peppers are not sticking by nudging them carefully and stirring the cooking juices with a spatula. Continue to cook slowly, checking on the peppers occasionally to prevent sticking and scorching, until they feel soft to the touch and the juices in the bottom of the pan have turned very richly brown, about 1 hour.

Remove the peppers with a spatula to a serving dish, still upside down. Stir the cooking juices in the pan, and then spoon the mixture over and around the peppers.

Serves 6

shanghainese slow-cooked chicken

3 large onions (about 2 pounds), coarsely chopped

¼ cup vegetable oil

8 chicken legs (about 3 pounds)

1 cup sesame-soy sauce (see page 24)

6 large eggs, hard boiled

Hot white rice for serving

I grew up eating this dish and now my daughter Ursula loves it so much she asks for it even on her birthday. My mother made it with pork chops but I use chicken drumsticks. You can use deboned legs or ask the butcher to cut off the bottom inch or so of the bone if you don't want to mess with it at home. Stew the chicken a day before serving to let its flavors develop. Plus, as it sits, the fat will separate and rise to the surface so it can be easily taken off. When I was a bachelor, I would make a big batch and freeze it. Then, when I got home late, I would defrost a portion while the rice cooked. The recipe calls for six eggs because the number six is lucky and the golden yolks symbolize wealth.

Heat a medium-size Dutch oven over medium heat and add the onions and oil. Stir well, cover, and cook until the onions are very soft, stirring occasionally, about 15 minutes.

Meanwhile, chop off the bottom knuckle of each drumstick with a cleaver or large knife, discard the bony pieces, and peel off the skin. Add the chicken and the sauce to the onions. Cover the pot and bring the mixture to a rapid boil. Adjust the heat to maintain a medium simmer and cook, stirring occasionally, about 15 minutes.

Peel the eggs and cut them in half lengthwise. Lay them gently in the pot and baste with the cooking liquid. Replace the cover and continue to simmer over low heat, basting every few minutes. When the eggs take on a mahogany color, after about 15 minutes, the stew is ready. Let it cool to allow the fat to rise to the surface. Pour off the fat and, when ready to serve, return the pot to low heat until the stew is hot through. Serve over rice.

Serves 4

skewered sesame chicken

So simple and so delicious. This recipe takes the idea of the popular Chinese stir-fry Mandarin beef and gives it an American application. Chicken and slices of fresh, unpeeled orange are threaded alternately onto skewers. The grilling caramelizes the orange peel, giving it an intensely sweet and savory flavor.

4 wooden skewers, soaked in water for several minutes

1 pound skinless, boneless chicken thighs

1 large navel orange, cut into ⅓-inch-thick slices, then quartered

½ cup sesame-soy sauce (see page 24)

Vegetable oil for brushing grill pan

Hot white rice for serving

Cut the chicken into about 1-inch chunks, trimming away any big pieces of fat. Thread the skewers though the orange peels and chicken alternately. Thread any leftover orange pieces onto a separate skewer.

Put the skewers on a large plate and pour the sauce over them. Turn to coat well. Let the chicken marinate at least 10 minutes and up to 24 hours in the refrigerator.

Preheat a grill to medium-high heat. Brush a wire rack or pan with oil. Grill the skewers, basting frequently with the marinade. Turn the skewers occasionally, basting all the while, until the chicken turns a deep mahogany color on all sides and is cooked through, about 12 minutes. Grill the skewer of orange pieces, if you have one, for the last few minutes of cooking.

To serve, slide the chicken and orange off the skewers and arrange on a platter. Squeeze the juice from the skewered orange pieces over the chicken. Serve hot with the rice.

Serves 4

chicken and pea pod stir-fry

This is a wonderful combination of tastes and sensations: sweet, salty, savory, crunchy, and tender. I like to add a visual and textural dimension to a dish by varying the size of the ingredients and sometimes the cutting style. Here, the chicken must be cut very thinly so it can quickly soak up the sauce flavors.

2 tablespoons vegetable oil

2 skinless, boneless chicken breasts, very thinly sliced across the grain

½ cup black bean sauce (see page 21)

12 ounces snow peas, topped and tailed

½ red bell pepper, cut into ⅛-inch dice

Heat the oil in a large flat-bottomed wok or sauté pan over medium-high heat. Add the chicken and stir vigorously. Add the sauce and stir and cook for about another minute. Add the snow peas and continue to stir and cook, keeping the contents of the pan moving, until the chicken is cooked through and the peas are crisp-tender, about 1 minute more. Scrape the contents of the pan onto a warm serving dish and garnish with the red pepper. Serve immediately.

Serves 4

slow-simmered star anise duck

1½ cups Star Anise Sauce
(page 36), divided

1 whole duck (about 4 pounds),
cut into 8 to 10 pieces

1 teaspoon cornstarch

¼ cup vegetable oil

4 very large onions
(about 3 pounds), coarsely
chopped

Hot white rice for serving

Poultry and star anise is a classic Chinese flavor combination; star anise is indigenous to China and, along with Chinese cassia (cinnamon), is one of the most common spices used. This dish has a subtle anise aroma and flavor that lasts long on the palate. The recipe is my interpretation of one of my aunt's. Hers takes three days of long, slow simmering and skimming. Mine cooks slowly but for only about one-and-a-half hours. It's best to cook this several hours to a day ahead of time. Let the duck cool in the sauce and absorb the juices. Then the fat will float to the surface and can then be easily poured off. Use the same method with beef shank. It's a great recipe for a crockpot.

Pour ¾ cup of the sauce over the duck in a shallow baking dish or bowl and set aside. Stir the cornstarch together with the remaining sauce in a small bowl and set aside.

Heat a large Dutch oven over medium heat and add the oil and onions. Cover and cook until the onions are soft, about 15 minutes. Stir occasionally.

Add the duck and its marinade to the pan and stir well. Cover and regulate the heat to maintain a slow simmer. After 30 minutes, add the cornstarch mixture in increments of ¼ cup every 15 minutes, stirring after each addition.

Cook until the duck is tender and cooked through and the sauce is a dark caramel color, about 1½ hours total. If the sauce does not look thick enough, remove the lid and simmer until the liquid is about the texture of heavy cream. Let the dish rest a few minutes to let the duck reabsorb the juices and to let the fat rise to the top. Pour off the fat and serve the duck over rice.

Serves 4 to 6

sesame-soy pork tenderloin

1 pork tenderloin (about 1 pound)

1 cup sesame-soy sauce
(see page 24)

Vegetable oil for brushing grill pan
(optional)

Sesame-soy is the cooking sauce for a Chinese braised dish of pork chops. Before I premade the sauce in large quantities, achieving the flavor took hours. When I gave my friends small bottles of the sauce, they used it to give their own style of cooking a new flavor, using it to grill, bake, and pour over plain rice. Try the sauce for grilling pork chops, flank steak, or even a butterflied leg of lamb. If you like citrus flavors with pork, add the zest of an orange to the marinade. Serve the pork with the Cherry Tomato and Cucumber Salad (page 60) and the Not-fried Rice (page 115).

Put the pork and sauce in a plastic bag, seal tightly, and agitate to coat the meat well with sauce. Let marinate for at least 30 minutes and up to 24 hours in the refrigerator.

Heat a nonstick grill pan over medium-high heat or preheat a grill to medium-high heat. Brush a wire rack or pan with oil if not using nonstick. Grill the meat, turning occasionally and basting frequently, until it is only a little pink inside, about 15 minutes. Remove from the heat a little underdone, as the meat will continue to cook as it rests.

Let the meat rest about 5 minutes, and then slice and serve.

Serves 4

barbecued pork short ribs

3 pounds pork short ribs, cut into individual ribs

2 cups Sweet Scallion Sauce (page 33)

Vegetable oil for brushing grill pan

Compared to those of other parts of China, Shanghainese menus include a good deal of meat. The amount of meat served reflects well on the wealth and prosperity of the household. And many Shanghainese families in the past, and again today, could afford meat. These ribs are meaty with a sweet, delicate flavor and they are very fast and easy to prepare. Scattering Fava Beans in Sweet Scallion Sauce (page 33) over the ribs on a platter makes a very pretty presentation.

Preheat a grill to medium-high heat. Meanwhile, put the ribs in a large pot and cover them with water. Bring to a boil over high heat and simmer for about 10 minutes. Drain off the water and pat the ribs dry with paper towels. In a large bowl, pour the sauce over the ribs and toss well. Marinate the ribs until they are cool or up to 24 hours in the refrigerator.

Brush a wire rack or grill pan with oil, and grill the ribs, basting them very frequently with the marinade, until the ribs are crusty and browned all over, about 15 minutes. Serve immediately.

Serves 3 to 4

curry beef

In Shanghai, my maternal grandfather lived next to a very wealthy family from India. When they prepared to leave during the Youth Rebellion, they went to my grandfather and asked him to take their home and protect it. But he had his own to worry about. They asked whether he would at least take their servants in and protect them. And that was how we came to eat curry on that side of our family. In my father's family, the bodyguards—all wealthy families had bodyguards to protect against kidnapping—were from Calcutta, and so our family preferred Calcutta-style curries. The dish has a rich, nutty flavor. You can also make it with chicken or lamb.

2 extra-large onions (about 1½ pounds), cut into ¼-inch dice

¼ cup vegetable oil

1½ pounds stew beef, cut into 1-inch cubes

3 tablespoons curry powder (see Note)

1 tablespoon tomato paste

2 teaspoons sugar

Salt

1 teaspoon sherry

¼ teaspoon cornstarch

¼ teaspoon freshly ground pepper

10 ounces baby carrots

1 pound baby potatoes

Heat a medium-size Dutch oven over medium heat and add the onions and oil. Stir well, cover, and cook until the onions are very soft, stirring occasionally, about 15 minutes.

Add the meat, curry powder, tomato paste, sugar, 1 teaspoon salt, sherry, cornstarch, and pepper to the pot, and mix well. Cover, and cook gently, stirring occasionally, until the meat is nearly tender, about 2 hours. Add the carrots and continue to cook until the carrots are about half tender, about 10 minutes.

Meanwhile, put the potatoes in a pot of water, season with salt, and bring to a boil. Cook until the potatoes are not quite tender, about 5 minutes. Drain the potatoes and let them cool. Cut them, if necessary, into even pieces, about 1 inch in size. Add the potatoes to the stew, and continue to simmer gently until the vegetables are cooked through and the meat is very tender. Taste and adjust the seasoning with salt.

Serves 4

Note: Calcutta-style curry powder is a popular Chinese ingredient, especially in Southern China. The popular Daw Sen's used to be available as a paste—and the paste is preferable to the powder—but I can't seem to find it anymore, even in Chinatown. The color of curry is important—the turmeric gives a golden yellow color and my mother would judge hers on whether it was red enough, adding more tomato paste until she had the color she wanted. If you can't find Daw Sen's, substitute any Indian curry powder that is easily available. Just make sure it is as fresh as possible. Rarely do people think to combine curry with other Asian sauces, but I encourage you to try sweet soy and peanut sauces with curry.

spicy pork and eggplant

About ¾ cup vegetable oil, divided

1¼ pounds ground pork

1¼ cups Shanghainese Red Pepper Sauce (page 34), divided

2 Japanese eggplants (about 1 pound), cut into ¼-inch-thick slices

If you cook the pork until all the fat and liquid have been removed—and this takes a long time of stirring and cooking—it will puff up like cotton. A small bowl of such pork would be put on the table as a condiment. This is a daily sort of dish, one that everyone seems to like, and so simple it makes a terrific weeknight supper.

Heat 2 tablespoons of the oil in a large flat-bottomed wok or sauté pan over low heat. Add the meat and stir to break up the lumps. Cook, stirring, until the meat is evenly gray and has released its water and fat. Drain off and discard the cooking liquids.

Increase the heat to medium-high, add 1 cup of the sauce, and cook while stirring constantly to coat the meat, about 8 minutes. Add another tablespoon of the oil and continue to cook, stirring continuously, about 5 more minutes. Add more oil, if needed, so the meat has a nice sheen to it, and to prevent the meat from sticking to the bottom of the pan.

In a separate large flat-bottomed wok or sauté pan, heat ½ cup of the oil over high heat. Add the eggplant and cook, stirring and tossing continuously, until it is just tender, about 3 minutes.

Add the pork to the eggplant and toss well. Add the remaining ¼ cup sauce, or to taste, to give the dish a shiny mahogany color.

Serves 4

red pepper beef and tofu stir-fry

12 ounces boneless rib-eye steak, trimmed of fat and cut into ⅛-inch-thick slices across the grain

1 cup Shanghainese Red Pepper Sauce (page 34), divided

½ cup plus 2 tablespoons vegetable oil, divided

14 ounces firm tofu, cut into pieces about ¼ inch thick and 2 inches square

Salt

¼ large red bell pepper, cut into ⅛-inch dice (optional)

The yang of beef balances the yin of tofu. Traditionally, this dish is made with silken tofu. It falls into soft, custard-like curds when cut. Then, when the beef is poured on top, the tofu melts and absorbs the flavors. Using silken tofu also saves a cooking step. I think most Americans prefer a firmer tofu. Cooking firm tofu until lightly browned gives it a good flavor and texture of its own. If you want to add a vegetable component, serve the beef over spinach with rice on the side or stir a fine chiffonade of Swiss chard into the meat during the last minute of cooking, just to wilt the chard.

In a small bowl, toss the meat with ½ cup of the sauce and set aside for about 5 minutes.

Heat ½ cup of the oil in a flat-bottomed wok or nonstick sauté pan over high heat. Add the tofu, sprinkle it lightly with salt, and cook, swirling the pan and stirring gently to prevent the tofu from sticking. Be careful not to break up the tofu. Keep moving and turning the tofu until it is lightly browned, about 7 minutes. Remove the tofu to a plate and keep warm in the oven on low heat.

In the same pan, heat the remaining 2 tablespoons oil over high heat. Scrape the meat and marinade into the pan. Add the remaining ½ cup sauce, or to taste, and quickly stir and cook until the meat is done but still rare, about 2 minutes. Immediately pour over the tofu and serve the dish garnished with diced red pepper, if desired.

Serves 4

sliced steak and mushroom stir-fry

Westerners cut their food at the table while Chinese cut every-thing beforehand and use chopsticks at the table, never knives. Chinese do not give gifts of knives because that would be sym-bolic of cutting someone's life short. Nor do we give clocks because then the recipient would watch their life go by. But no time at all is needed for this recipe. Black bean sauce and beef were made for each other.

1 tablespoon vegetable oil

8 ounces filet mignon, market steak (boneless rib-eye), or sirloin steak, diagonally cut into very thin slices

⅓ cup black bean sauce (see page 20)

4 ounces button mushrooms, thinly sliced

Heat the oil in a large flat-bottomed wok or sauté pan over high heat. Add the meat, stirring and tossing very fast. Working quickly, add the sauce, stir, and then add the mushrooms. Stir and cook until the meat is rare and the mushrooms barely begin to wilt, about 1½ minutes more.

Serves 4

black bean–grilled flank steak

1 cup black bean sauce
(see page 20)

1 pound flank steak

Vegetable oil for brushing grill pan

1 red bell pepper, cut into a very
fine julienne

"That should be illegal," said one of our tasters when we tested
this recipe, because it tasted so good. You probably would not
identify it as Chinese; it just tastes great. The red peppers
add crunch and juiciness. If you toss them together while the
meat is hot, the peppers will wilt just a little bit, taking the
raw edge off them. For a jubilee of colors, use red, green, and
yellow bell peppers.

Scrape the black bean sauce into a medium bowl or deep plate and
turn the steak in the sauce until it is well coated. Marinate for at
least 30 minutes and up to 24 hours in the refrigerator.

Preheat a grill to medium-high heat. Brush a wire rack or pan with
oil. Grill the steak, basting constantly with the marinade, until it
is brown on the first side, about 2 minutes. Turn and continue
basting with marinade. Prick the steak all over with a sharp knife or
the prongs of a fork. Continue to grill until the meat is nicely
browned on all sides and done to your preference, about 7 minutes
for rare.

Remove the steak from the heat and let it rest a few minutes. Carve
across the grain into very thin slices. Toss the meat and the red
pepper together in a medium bowl or on a serving platter and serve
immediately. Or, arrange the peppers on a serving plate and then
arrange the meat over the top.

Serves 4

fish and shellfish

sweet scallion shrimp

16 to 20 large shrimp
(about 1 pound), tail on, peeled
and deveined

Salt

Cornstarch for dusting

About 3 tablespoons dry sherry

¼ to ½ cup Sweet Scallion Sauce
(page 33)

1 pint basket cherry tomatoes
(optional)

On my own, I would never have thought of pairing Sweet Scallion Sauce with shrimp, but I am glad my dear friend Alison South did for a holiday dinner. Serve the shrimp as an appetizer and it will disappear like candy. Or thread the shrimp onto skewers with cherry tomatoes, brush with the sauce, and grill, then serve them with Tangy Ginger Sauce (page 30) as a dip. This makes a terrific pasta dish, too. Toss cooked pasta with a little Sweet Scallion Sauce and add peas and cherry tomatoes to the shrimp for the last minute of cooking. Then toss everything together and serve immediately. You can also substitute halibut for the shrimp in this recipe.

Put the shrimp in a colander, sprinkle them with a pinch of salt, and toss lightly. Sprinkle on a large pinch of cornstarch and toss again, then splash the sherry over the shrimp and shake off the excess.

Heat a flat-bottomed wok or sauté pan over high heat and add ¼ cup of the sauce. Immediately add the shrimp. Cook rapidly, stirring and tossing the shrimp until they are pink and cooked through, about 3 minutes. The shrimp should move easily in the pan and sizzle. If using the tomatoes, add them in the last 15 to 30 seconds of cooking, just to warm them through. If the pan is too dry, add more sauce by the tablespoonful. Serve immediately.

Serves 4

grilled scallion–ginger salmon

Salt

Four 6-ounce salmon fillets

Scant ½ teaspoon cornstarch

About ⅓ cup sesame-soy sauce
(see page 24)

¼ cup toasted sesame oil

4 scallions, white and green parts,
thinly sliced

2 tablespoons minced peeled fresh
ginger, preferably baby ginger

2 tablespoons sugar

This is one of my favorite family recipes. I used to make up the sauce ingredients in large batches to save time. It's terrific drizzled on steamed white fish just before serving and for steamed green beans, too. To grill a whole salmon, make a "boat" of heavy-duty aluminum foil to lay the fish in. Then baste it frequently with the sauce while it cooks. When shopping for this dish, ask for fillets from the tail of the fish. This is where the action is for a fish, so that is where the most flavor is.

Lightly salt both sides of the fillets, let rest in a colander for about 10 minutes, and then pat dry with paper towels. Place in a shallow baking dish.

Stir the cornstarch together with the sauce in a small bowl and set aside. Heat the oil in a small sauté pan over low heat. Add the scallions and sauté until they are fragrant, about 30 seconds. Stir in the ginger and cook until blended, about 1 minute. Whisk the cornstarch mixture again, and then add it with the sugar to the pan. Stir until smooth and blended. Bring the mixture to a boil over medium-high heat and simmer until it is slightly thickened.

Pour the scallion-ginger sauce over the fillets. Turn to coat both sides well and set them aside for another 10 to 15 minutes.

Place the fillets, skin-side down, on an unheated, nonstick grill pan, and heat over medium heat, until beginning to sizzle, about 5 minutes. Place a splatter guard over the pan, if you have one. Reduce the heat to medium-low, allowing the fillets to cook slowly from the bottom up.

As the fillets cook, the juices bubble up to the surface and coagulate, giving a good visual cue to doneness. After about 15 minutes, white juices will begin to rise up to the top of the fillets, indicating that they are cooked through. (Timing will depend on both the thickness of your fillets and the heat of the pan.) Turn the fillets over and cook the second sides just until brown. Turn again, baste with some of the scallion-ginger sauce, then turn again to caramelize the tops. Remove the fillets to warm plates or a platter and keep warm.

Bring any remaining sauce to a boil in a small pan over high heat. Pour over the fillets and serve immediately.

Serves 4

spicy chili bean scallops

1 tablespoon vegetable oil

1 pound bay scallops

Salt

Cornstarch for dusting

About 3 tablespoons dry sherry

1 cup Spicy Chili Bean Sauce
(page 34)

4 large handfuls (about 4 ounces)
fresh spinach

When I create a dish, I try to enhance the natural flavor of the main ingredient. Scallops are sweet. I don't want to change that, but add to it. The bean sauce sets off the sweetness with spice and depth of flavor. These are addictive—sweet and spicy. With rice, they make a meal.

Heat the oil in a large flat-bottomed wok or sauté pan over medium-high heat. Meanwhile, put the scallops in a colander, sprinkle them with a large pinch of salt, and toss lightly. Sprinkle on a large pinch of cornstarch and toss again, then splash the sherry over the scallops and shake off the excess.

Add the scallops to the hot pan, stirring and tossing them. Add the sauce and stir and toss continuously until the scallops are cooked through, about 3 minutes.

Divide the spinach among 4 plates, and then spoon the scallops and sauce beside the spinach.

Serves 4

Note: Often fish and shellfish—even that just brought home from the market—is less than pristine. It might smell not quite fresh, for instance. To return the fish to a neutral state where it smells and tastes fresh and sweet, I use a technique my mother taught me. First sprinkle the fish with a pinch of salt and then, for shellfish, a pinch of cornstarch. Then toss the seafood with some dry sherry and immediately shake off the excess. I prefer, if possible, to salt my fish up to a day ahead of time, especially if grilling. The salting removes water and gives the fish a little "cure," allowing it to soak up more flavor when cooked.

sea bass with country ham, scallions, and ginger

4 tablespoons vegetable oil, divided

4 sea bass fillets (4 to 6 ounces each)

Salt

About ⅓ cup dry sherry

3 fat scallions, white and green parts, thinly sliced

½ cup prepared minced ginger (see page 22) or finely minced baby ginger

1½ ounces smoked country ham such as Smithfield, very finely chopped

This dish is traditionally made with a whole steamed fish and served at the end of a meal to signify abundance. If you like steamed fish, try steaming the fillets in this recipe; I like them that way. I've added no salt or sugar here. The sweetness comes naturally from the scallions and ginger, while the ham provides the salt flavor.

Heat 2 tablespoons of the oil in a large flat-bottomed wok or sauté pan over low heat. Meanwhile, put the fillets in a colander, sprinkle with a little salt, and then toss with the sherry. Shake off the excess. Immediately add the fillets to the wok. Cook until opaque throughout, about 7 minutes, turning once when the edges begin to brown.

While the fillets are cooking, heat the remaining 2 tablespoons oil in a separate sauté pan over high heat. Add the scallions and ginger. Cook and stir until the scallions are very soft, about 3 minutes. Add the ham and toss and cook until the ham is heated through and slightly browned, about 3 minutes.

When the fillets are done, arrange on warm plates or a serving platter, and scrape the ham mixture over the top. Serve immediately.

Serves 4

clams in black bean sauce

2 pounds clams, preferably small Manila clams

4 tablespoons vegetable oil, divided

⅔ cup black bean sauce (see page 20)

A friend called me once because he was trying to recreate his favorite Chinese dish—clams with black beans. He had purchased dried black turtle beans. You make black bean chili with turtle beans; you make black bean sauce with Chinese dried, salted black beans. These are actually salted, fermented soy beans (see page 21). With a bottle of black bean sauce in the pantry, this dish goes together in a minute. It makes a great opener to a dinner party. As everyone licks the sauce from their fingers, conversation flows.

Put the clams in a colander, and rinse them well with cold water. Discard any that are open.

Heat 2 tablespoons of the oil in a flat-bottomed wok or large sauté pan over high heat. Add the clams, tossing and turning them and stirring occasionally, and cook until they pop open, about 3 minutes. Larger clams will take longer to open. Make sure to throw away any that do not open.

Add the remaining 2 tablespoons oil and the sauce to the clams and stir until they are coated and the sauce is hot, about 1 minute. Serve immediately.

Serves 4

rock shrimp with spinach

Shanghai is famous for a dish called "Drunken Shrimp." Live shrimp are marinated in Shaoxing, a sherry-like rice wine, and then eaten while still alive. It's a sort of Chinese ceviche. You can substitute halibut for the shrimp, but pan-fry the fish and lay it over the spinach, then warm the sauce and pour it over the top. Timing seafood can be tricky because it so easily overcooks and gets dry. I tend to cook it just until barely done. Then it finishes cooking on its way to the table.

4 tablespoons vegetable oil, divided

10 ounces spinach

2 teaspoons Asian Salad Dressing

1 pound rock shrimp, peeled and deveined

Salt

Cornstarch for dusting

About 3 tablespoons dry sherry

½ cup Spicy Chili Bean Sauce (page 34)

Heat 2 tablespoons of the oil in a medium flat-bottomed wok or sauté pan over high heat. Add the spinach and sauté just until it is wilted, about 30 seconds. Arrange the spinach on a plate and toss it with the dressing. Set aside.

Put the shrimp in a colander, sprinkle with a pinch of salt, and toss lightly. Sprinkle on a large pinch of cornstarch and toss again, then splash the sherry over the shrimp and shake off the excess.

In the same wok in which the spinach cooked, heat the remaining 2 tablespoons oil over medium-high heat. Add the shrimp, stir and toss, and add the sauce. Stir and cook until the shrimp are just barely cooked through, about 2 minutes more. Scrape the shrimp over the spinach and serve immediately or at room temperature.

Serves 4

vegetables, rice, and noodles

braised mushrooms and pepper strips with tofu

2 ounces dried Chinese black mushrooms (see page 21)

½ cup vegetable oil, divided

10 baby carrots, cut into matchstick-size pieces

3 bell peppers (green, yellow and red), thinly julienned

2 teaspoons salt, divided

½ teaspoon sugar

9 ounces baked, seasoned (soy or five-spice flavor) or plain, firm tofu, cut into matchstick-size pieces

Dried mushrooms are a common gift at the Chinese New Year. They symbolize prosperity because, when put in water, they swell, or grow. So by giving dried mushrooms to a business associate, you indicate that you wish that their business prospers in the coming year. A mushroom's quality is judged by how "fat," or thick, the cap is. The fatter it is, the better the quality. I use dried Chinese black mushrooms, but you could also use shiitake, fresh or dried, or a combination of mushrooms. This dish is a labor of love because the vegetables require so much preparation. But it is best when made ahead and given several hours to develop its flavor. Use green, yellow, and red peppers together to add color.

Soak the mushrooms in 3 cups of water in a medium bowl for at least 1 hour. Strain, reserving the mushroom-soaking liquid. Remove the stems and cut the mushrooms into ¼-inch-thick slices.

Heat ¼ cup of the oil in a large flat-bottomed wok or sauté pan over medium heat. Add 1 cup of the mushroom-soaking liquid, then stir in the carrots and bring to a simmer.

Add the peppers and another ½ cup mushroom-soaking liquid, and return the mixture to a lively simmer. Cook until the peppers begin to wilt. Stir in 1½ teaspoons of the salt.

continued

Add the mushrooms and cook, stirring occasionally, for about another 4 minutes. Stir in the sugar, and then fold in the tofu. Add the remaining ¼ cup oil, if desired. Cook and stir to allow the flavors to meld and the vegetables to cook through, about 2 minutes. Taste and adjust the seasoning with the remaining ½ teaspoon salt, if needed.

Pour the mixture into a deep serving bowl or platter, wrap it with plastic wrap to capture the steam and further enhance the flavors, and let the mixture cool. Serve at room temperature.

Serves 6

sweet soy–sauced broccolini

1 bunch broccolini
(about 8 ounces), well trimmed

About 2 tablespoons Sweet Soy
Sauce (page 35)

In Shanghai, we would drizzle Chinese broccoli with toasted sesame oil and soy sauce. The Cantonese would use oyster sauce. But I have found that people are at first surprised at and then fall in love with the combination of a sweetened soy sauce and green vegetables such as broccolini, asparagus, and green beans. The best part of broccolini is the stems, so be sure to trim them well. Serve this as a side dish to a spicy beef.

In the bottom of a large steamer, bring water to a boil. Add the broccolini and steam until the color brightens and the stalks are just tender, about 4 minutes.

Arrange the broccolini on a plate. Drizzle the sauce over the stems and serve them immediately or at room temperature.

Serves 4

fava beans in sweet scallion sauce

½ cup Sweet Scallion Sauce
(page 33)

1 pound fresh fava beans, shelled
and peeled if necessary

I can hardly wait for early summer to arrive because it brings
with it my favorite dish, fava beans in a sauce made with lots
of scallions that intensify the sweet taste of the small fresh
beans. If you choose the youngest, most tender beans, you do
not have to peel off their inner skins. You can substitute other
vegetables, such as green peas, sugar snaps, snow peas, soybeans,
or fresh lima beans. Make sure to serve rice.

Bring the sauce to a gentle bubble in a large flat-bottomed wok or
sauté pan over medium heat. Add the beans and simmer gently just
until they are cooked through, about 5 minutes. Serve hot or warm.

Serves 4 to 6

shanghainese asparagus

1 pound asparagus, trimmed

2 tablespoons toasted sesame oil

¼ cup soy sauce

The two basic flavors of Chinese cooking are soy and sesame. It's that simple. Together, they make a wonderful sauce for steamed or sautéed vegetables. Even though the asparagus is served at room temperature, I would serve it with hot rice as a first course or side dish to a roast chicken.

In the bottom of a large steamer, bring water to a boil. Add the asparagus and steam until the color brightens and the stalks are just tender, about 5 minutes, depending on the thickness of the asparagus.

Meanwhile, whisk together the oil and soy sauce in a small bowl. Arrange the asparagus on a platter, and drizzle the sesame-soy dressing over the spears. Let them sit to absorb the flavors, about 10 minutes. Serve at room temperature.

Serves 4

soybeans with salted cabbage

¼ cup vegetable oil

1 pound frozen, shelled soybeans

5 ounces salted snow cabbage
(see Note)

Salt

This is what comfort food tastes like in my family. I have eaten this dish my whole life and particularly love it cold with a bowl of hot rice. You can add sliced mushrooms to the pan with the soybeans to just wilt into the dish. Another traditional addition is rehydrated bean curd sheets. They break up naturally in the warmth of the dish. In my experience, frozen soybeans tend to go brown if defrosted before cooking, so I toss them directly from the freezer bag into the hot pan. Cook them just until warmed through.

Heat the oil in a large flat-bottomed wok or sauté pan over high heat. Add the soybeans and cook, stirring occasionally, until the beans begin to defrost and warm, about 2 minutes. Add the cabbage and salt to taste, and continue to cook and stir until the beans are hot through, about another 2 minutes.

Serve warm, at room temperature, or cold with hot rice.

Serves 4

Variation: A great addition is ½ to 1 ounce dried Chinese black mushrooms (see page 21), rehydrated and sliced. Add them and some of their soaking liquid to the pan with the cabbage.

Note: You can find vacuum-sealed packages of salted snow cabbage in the refrigerated section of Asian groceries. It is dark green and has a slight crunch. And Western palates do not need to fear its flavor: It is not at all funky, but instead has a savory, subtle cabbage flavor. Kim chi's flavor is too garlicky to substitute here, but you can use fresh sauerkraut or balance the stronger flavor of supermarket jarred sauerkraut by adding 1 ounce dried Chinese black mushrooms, as above.

five-flavored silken tofu

1 pound silken tofu or firm tofu

⅓ cup toasted sesame oil

½ cup soy sauce

1 to 3 tablespoons Spicy Chili Bean Sauce (page 34)

1¼ ounces pickled mustard greens (preserved radish), cut into ⅛-inch dice (about ¼ cup; see Note)

1 ounce dried shrimp, minced

Many families eat a version of this traditional Shanghai dish for breakfast as one of several dishes served with rice porridge. I also love its clean flavors at lunch with a bowl of rice. Silken tofu has a wonderful smooth, flan-like texture. If preserved mustard greens and dried shrimp are a little too exotic, the dish is still wonderful without them. You could substitute smoked salmon or prosciutto for the shrimp. Chopped, salted peanuts would be another traditional Chinese garnish.

Carefully unpack the tofu onto a deep plate and blot with paper towels. Cut into ½-inch cubes.

Whisk together the oil and soy sauce in a small bowl and pour it over the tofu.

Spoon on 1 or more tablespoons of the bean sauce, to taste, and then scatter the mustard greens and shrimp over the top. Spoon the dressing from around the tofu and pour over the dish to distribute evenly.

Serves 4

Note: You will find canned, preserved radish (mustard greens) in Asian groceries. The ingredient label will say "pickled radish with chili and spices." They are a type of collard or mustard green. You can sometimes find these freshly pickled, but I prefer the stronger flavor of the canned. Slice and cut the vegetable into small dice to scatter over dishes that would benefit from a salty crunch.

sautéed sweet pea shoots

1 tablespoon vegetable oil

4 thin slices fresh ginger

6 ounces sweet pea shoots

1 teaspoon dry sherry

Salt

3 tablespoons rendered chicken fat or duck fat, divided

Sweet green pea shoots have been eaten as a seasonal delicacy in China forever. But their delicate, sweet flavor is still unknown to many Westerners. The shoots have, however, leapt over the boundaries of Chinatowns and can be found on restaurant menus and in specialty markets. And they have proven so popular that the shoots are now grown as a crop instead of being available only as a delicious by-product of sweet peas. Great food is not about the most expensive ingredients. It is about how ingredients are handled and combined to enhance essential flavors. This recipe of my grandmother's is an example of that principle. Everyone, from my grandfather's peers to my buddies who would devour anything she had made, agreed that my grandmother's cooking was the best.

Heat the oil in a flat-bottomed wok or large sauté pan over high heat. Add the ginger and sauté until fragrant. Add the pea shoots, sherry, and a pinch of salt. Cook and stir vigorously to allow the flavors to meld and the vegetables to just wilt, about 1½ minutes. Add 2 tablespoons of the chicken fat to the pan and stir to distribute evenly.

Quickly slide the shoots out of the pan onto a plate, and add the remaining tablespoon chicken fat to the pan and melt it. Drizzle the fat over the shoots and serve immediately.

Serves 4

not-fried rice

½ medium head iceberg lettuce, shredded (about 4 cups)

About 3 cups cooked jasmine rice, warm

4 large eggs

Salt

4 tablespoons vegetable oil, divided

6 ounces frozen green peas

1¼ ounces smoked country ham such as Smithfield, cut into ⅛-inch dice

Fried rice was originally a dish cooked by servants. They reheated and stretched leftovers from the master's table by tossing them together with rice in a wok. Cantonese use soy for the salt flavor, so their fried rice is brown. In Shanghai, fried rice is white because we use table salt. The simple soothing flavors and pretty colors make this a great dish for kids of all ages. Add any vegetables you happen to have on hand, such as diced bell peppers, carrots, corn, and soybeans. Rarely does a Western kitchen have day-old rice, but dried-out rice is important because it will soak up the oil and flavorings. You don't need to start a day ahead. Just cook the rice with a little less water than usual.

In a large serving bowl, mix together the lettuce and rice. The rice should be warm enough to wilt the lettuce slightly. You may need to microwave the rice if it is a day old.

In a small bowl, lightly beat the eggs and a pinch of salt together with a fork. Heat 2 tablespoons of the oil in a large flat-bottomed wok or sauté pan over medium heat. Add the eggs and softly scramble to form soft curds. Scrape the eggs into the bowl with the rice and toss gently.

Add another tablespoon of the oil to the pan and return it to medium-high heat. Add the peas and salt to taste and heat through, about 2 minutes. Add the peas to the bowl and toss again.

Return the pan to medium-high heat and add the remaining 1 tablespoon of the oil. When hot, add the ham and cook until is hot through, about 1 minute. Add the ham to the bowl and toss well. Taste and adjust the seasoning with salt. Serve at room temperature.

Serves 6

sweet and sour rice

2½ cups cooked short-grain white rice (see Note)

½ cup toasted, sliced almonds

½ cup dried cranberries

½ cup soybeans, green peas, or lima beans

¼ cup (plus more if desired) Asian Salad Dressing

Salt

Freshly ground white pepper

There is a Chinese expression for people who eat what is considered too much rice: Rice Head. It means you don't appreciate great food, because you fill yourself up with rice. It's like eating all the bread at a great restaurant and killing your appetite for dinner. My family laughs at me because I love rice so much and love rice salads, too. This salad has an innocently addictive, clean, sweet, and tart flavor. I like to use short-grain white rice for a rice salad so it holds together and doesn't fall off your fork or chopsticks. The Cantonese often use short-grain rice to make a delicious fried rice that includes Chinese sausage, dried shrimp, mushrooms, and peas.

In a serving bowl, toss together the rice, almonds, cranberries, and soybeans. Carefully add the dressing, at first by tablespoonfuls and then by teaspoonfuls, tossing well and tasting after each addition. (Adjust the amout of dressing if desired.) Season to taste with salt and white pepper.

To mold the rice, press the salad into a ½ cup mold. Upend on a plate and the rice should release in its molded form. If not, firmly tap the bottom of the cup. You don't want to press the salad into the mold too tightly—the salad should hold together with all the ingredients remaining distinct.

Serves 4

Note: People often ask me what to serve with a dish. My answer is always the same—rice. We serve even cold dishes with hot rice. It makes an ideal neutral foil for all flavors. For daily use, choose a long-grain, aromatic white rice such as jasmine. At the supermarket, especially in the Asian food aisle, you will find short-grain white rice. It is slightly sticky and I use it for rice salads. It is not the same as Japanese "sweet" rice, also called sticky or glutinous rice.

spicy shrimp chow mein

12 ounces small or medium shrimp, peeled and deveined

Salt

Cornstarch for dusting

About 3 tablespoons dry sherry

About 8 tablespoons vegetable oil, divided

12 ounces dried Chinese noodles (see page 21) or fettuccine

2 to 3 scallions, white and green parts, thinly sliced

¼ cup Spicy Chili Bean Sauce (page 34)

About 2 tablespoons roasted, salted, shelled peanuts (optional)

Noodles—the longer the better—signify long life. They are traditionally served on your birthday as the final course. They are never cut before cooking because that might symbolize cutting life short. But when you eat noodles, you can use your teeth. And it is polite to slurp them. You can use any type of noodle you like for this dish. Both lo mein and chow mein are noodle dishes in which the noodles are stir-fried. The difference is the degree of browning. For chow mein, it is important to cook the noodles until they get well browned without getting dried out.

Put the shrimp in a colander, sprinkle with a pinch of salt, and toss lightly. Sprinkle on a large pinch of cornstarch and toss again, then splash the sherry over the shrimp and shake off the excess.

Bring a large pot of water to a boil, and add a large pinch of salt and 1 tablespoon of the oil. Add the noodles and cook until they are still chewy, about 3 minutes for thin Chinese noodles. Drain and rinse quickly with hot water. Drain again and reserve.

Heat 2 tablespoons of the oil in a large flat-bottomed wok or sauté pan over high heat. Add the scallions and cook until they begin to go limp. Add the shrimp, and stir and toss continuously, cooking until the shrimp are pink and not quite cooked through, about 2 minutes. Add the sauce and toss well until the shrimp are well coated and cooked through. Set aside.

In a separate wok or sauté pan, heat another 2 tablespoons of the oil over high heat. Add the noodles, and pat into a pancake. Let them cook, without moving them, until they brown on the bottom. Then begin turning and tossing them continuously, until the noodles have many browned and crusty parts, about 10 minutes. Add more oil by tablespoonfuls if the noodles begin to stick. They are done when they are loose, do not cling together, and are well browned.

Turn the noodles out onto a serving platter and top with the shrimp. Garnish with peanuts, if desired. Serve immediately or at room temperature.

Serves 4

spicy pork and cucumber

This is a traditional summer dish. It layers sweet, spicy, cool, and crunchy flavors and textures. Pork is used in the classic recipe, or you can use ground turkey thighs. Serving this with a shrimp dish would be a classic Chinese combination.

3 tablespoons vegetable oil, divided

1 pound ground pork

1 cup Shanghainese Red Pepper Sauce (page 34)

Salt

8 ounces flat, dried, Chinese noodles (see page 21)

3 tablespoons toasted sesame oil

5 tablespoons soy sauce

1 large cucumber (about 1 pound), peeled, seeded, and cut into ¼-inch dice

Heat 2 tablespoons of the vegetable oil in a flat-bottomed wok or sauté pan over medium-high heat and add the pork. Stir with a wooden spoon to break the meat into small bits. A splatter guard is helpful here.

Cook for several minutes until the meat releases its fat and juices. Pour off and discard the cooking liquid, and then add the sauce and stir well. Reduce the heat to maintain a rapid simmer and continue to cook, stirring well, until the pan is nearly dry and the meat is a reddish-mahogany color, about 20 minutes.

Meanwhile, bring a large pot of water to a boil, and add a large pinch of salt and the remaining 1 tablespoon of the vegetable oil. Add the noodles and cook until they are still chewy, about 5 minutes. Drain and rinse quickly with hot water. Drain again and transfer the noodles to a deep platter or large serving bowl.

Whisk together the sesame oil and soy sauce in a small bowl, and then pour half of the mixture over the warm noodles. Toss gently to coat well and let rest for several minutes. Toss the noodles well again with the remaining sesame-soy mixture until they are evenly moist and brown.

Pour and scrape the pork on top of the noodles, and then scatter the cucumbers over all. Serve at room temperature.

Serves 4

black mushrooms, scallions, and dried shrimp with noodles

2 ounces dried Chinese black mushrooms (see page 21)

Boiling water

1½ ounces small dried shrimp, whole or minced, as desired (see Note)

¼ cup dry sherry

3 tablespoons soy sauce

1 tablespoon plus 1 teaspoon toasted sesame oil

Salt

8 tablespoons vegetable oil, divided

6 ounces thin, dried, Chinese noodles (see page 21)

4 thin slices fresh ginger

1 large bunch scallions, white and green parts, thinly sliced (about 2 cups)

Sugar

This was my father's favorite dish and became mine as well. My mother would make it for me each time I left home for school. After my first attempts at cooking at school when I burned everything, my aunt sent me jars of the scallion, mushroom, and dried shrimp mixture so all I had to do was boil noodles. Some years later, when I was learning to cook, I asked my mother why my attempts were never as good as hers. She asked me what I used to soak the dried shrimp. "Water," I said. "No, dry sherry," she said, and a great mystery was solved. Even in families, recipes vary; my mother's version of this dish uses soy for the salt flavor; my grandmother's, as presented here, uses salt.

Put the mushrooms in a medium bowl, pour boiling water over them, and set aside until fully rehydrated, about 1 hour. Drain, remove the stems, and reserve the stems and the soaking liquid for stock. Cut the caps into ¼-inch-thick slices.

Meanwhile, marinate the shrimp in the sherry in a small cup or bowl. Whisk together the soy sauce and sesame oil in another small bowl and set aside.

Bring a large pot of water to a boil. Add a large pinch of salt, 1 table-spoon of the vegetable oil, and then the noodles. Cook until the noodles are still chewy, about 5 minutes. Drain and rinse quickly with hot water. Drain again and transfer the noodles to a deep platter or large serving bowl.

Heat the remaining 7 tablespoons of the vegetable oil in a flat-bottomed wok or large sauté pan over medium heat. Add the ginger and scallions and cook at a lively simmer until the scallions are very soft, about 5 minutes. Add the shrimp and their soaking liquid and stir. When the mixture returns to a consistent, lively simmer, after about 2 minutes, add the mushrooms and a pinch of sugar and stir. Cook until all the flavors have melded and everything is hot throughout and sizzling, about 5 minutes.

Remove from the heat and discard the ginger. Whisk the sesame oil and soy sauce again and stir it into the shrimp mixture. Immediately scrape the shrimp-mushroom mixture on top of the noodles and toss very well. Serve warm or at room temperature.

Serves 4

Note: As always, feel free to adjust the amounts of ingredients to your taste. If you are leery of dried shrimp, cut down on the amount or leave them out entirely.

chinese spaghetti

1 ounce dried Chinese black mushrooms

Boiling water

½ ounce dried shrimp

2 teaspoons dry sherry

½ cup sweet bean paste (see Note)

⅓ cup chili sauce (see page 20)

1 tablespoon hot bean paste (see page 20, optional)

1 tablespoon chili oil (see page 20)

1 teaspoon sugar

1 teaspoon toasted sesame oil

Salt

4 tablespoons vegetable oil, divided

1 pound thin, dried, Chinese noodles (see page 21) or angel hair pasta

4 ounces pork loin, cut into ¼-inch dice

4 ounces seasoned or five-spice baked tofu, cut into ¼-inch dice

¾ cup frozen, shelled soybeans

½ cup bamboo shoots, cut into ¼-inch dice (see Note on page 59)

I would often tell my grandmother to forget buying me a birthday present; all I wanted was a large jar of her Chinese spaghetti. If I went on a business trip, I could be sure my roommates would polish it all off. It surprised me because I think of this as typically Chinese in flavor. But its flavor is Shanghainese, delicately layered, and not very spicy. If you like more spice, simply add more chili oil or chili sauce to your taste. Grandmother serves this with flat noodles because she feels they balance the chunkiness of the other ingredients, but I prefer thin noodles. You, too, can use your favorite noodles.

Put the mushrooms in a medium bowl, pour boiling water over them, and set aside until fully reydrated, about 1 hour. Drain, remove the stems, and cut the caps into ¼-inch-thick slices. Set aside.

In a small bowl, mix together the shrimp and sherry, and set aside while you prepare the remaining ingredients. Then mince the shrimp, reserving them and their soaking liquid.

In a medium bowl, mix together the sweet bean paste, chili sauce, hot bean paste, chili oil, sugar, and sesame oil until smooth. Set aside.

Bring a pot of water to a boil, and add a large pinch of salt and 1 tablespoon of the oil. Add the noodles and cook until they are still chewy, about 3 minutes. Drain and rinse quickly with hot water. Drain again and transfer the noodles to a deep platter or large serving bowl.

continued

Heat the remaining 3 tablespoons of the vegetable oil in a large flat-bottomed wok or sauté pan over high heat. Working quickly, add the pork and toss. Stir in about ⅓ of the bean paste-chili mixture, and toss to coat the meat well. Add the mushrooms, stir and toss, and add another ⅓ of the chili mixture. Add the shrimp and their soaking liquid, the tofu, soybeans, and bamboo shoots. Stir and toss continuously until all the ingredients are cooked and heated through. Taste and adjust the seasoning with more of the chili mixture. Pour and scrape the meat and vegetables on top of the noodles and serve hot or at room temperature.

Serves 4

Note: Sweet bean paste has sugar added. It can be found in Chinatown, or simply add a little sugar to a purchased plain (no chilies!) bean paste. Bean pastes are made from salted, fermented beans such as black beans and broad beans. The beans are frequently ground to give the paste a smooth texture.

peanut-tossed noodles

My grandfather used to tell me that back in the 1700s and 1800s, his family lived almost at the top of the Soochow Mountains. The farmers at the base of the mountain grew peanuts and that is how the family came to incorporate them into their recipes. Peanuts were already prevalent in China, having arrived in the sixteenth century. When we came to America in the 1960s, we loved going to Sears, where they had a peanut roastery in the center of the store. We often had a small dish of roasted salted peanuts on the table at breakfast and dinner to use as a condiment. You can turn this combination into an entrée by tossing the cucumbers with the peanut sauce, arranging the chicken on top, and serving the dish with rice.

Salt

3 tablespoons vegetable oil, divided

8 ounces flat, dried, Chinese noodles (see page 21)

1¼ cups peanut sauce (see page 00)

Red pepper flakes (optional)

1 large cucumber, peeled, seeded, and cut into 2-inch-long by ¼-inch-thick pieces

One 6-ounce skinless, boneless chicken breast, sliced very thinly across the grain

½ cup Sweet Soy Sauce (page 23)

Bring a large pot of water to a boil. Add a large pinch of salt and 1 tablespoon of the oil. Add the noodles and cook until they are still chewy, about 5 minutes. Drain and rinse quickly in hot water. Drain again and transfer the noodles to a deep platter or bowl.

Add the peanut sauce and toss well so the noodles absorb the sauce. If the sauce you have is not spicy and you like spice, sprinkle the noodles with a pinch of red pepper flakes and toss again. Add the cucumbers and toss again.

Heat the remaining 2 tablespoons of the oil in a medium flat-bottomed wok or sauté pan over medium-high heat. Add the chicken and stir and toss for about 30 seconds.

Add the sauce and stir and cook quickly until the chicken is glossy and cooked through, about 2 minutes. Toss the noodles again, and then pour and scrape the chicken on top of the noodles. Serve warm or at room temperature.

Serves 3 to 4

desserts

tangy ginger bananas

¾ cup Tangy Ginger Sauce
(page 30)

½ cup packed brown sugar

2 large bananas, thickly sliced

Vanilla ice cream

My friend James Wierzelewski, now the Executive Chef of Vix's in South Beach, Miami, helped me create these bananas several years ago. They combine a sophisticated, intensely sweet/tart taste with the warm, comforting appeal of a nursery dessert. And they take only minutes to prepare. They are delicious over pound cake or gingerbread. In the summer, substitute peaches or nectarines, and in the fall, make the recipe with apples and pears.

Heat the sauce and sugar in a medium flat-bottomed wok or sauté pan over high heat. Bring to a rapid simmer, stirring well to dissolve the sugar, and reduce the mixture until it thickens slightly, about 3 minutes.

Add the bananas and stir, coating the fruit with the sauce. Return the mixture to a rapid simmer, and cook until the slices are cooked through, about 1 minute more.

Scoop the ice cream into 4 bowls and divide the hot bananas and sauce among them. Serve immediately.

Serves 4

Variation: You can make a similar dessert with fresh pineapple. Buy a 1-pound package of cubed pineapple or cut a large pineapple into rings or cubes. Pour about 1 cup Tangy Ginger Sauce over the pineapple in a bowl and marinate it in the refrigerator for at least 30 minutes. Grill or broil the pineapple, basting frequently with the marinade, until the fruit is browned on both sides and cooked through, about 10 minutes. Cook the remaining marinade in a small pan over high heat until it is syrupy. Serve as above, replacing the bananas with the grilled pineapple.

With clean beaters, beat the egg whites in another large bowl until soft peaks form. Gently stir half the whites into the batter, and then very gently fold in the remaining whites. Spoon and scrape the batter into the baking pan and smooth it over the pineapple.

Bake until the cake feels just firm in the center and a thin-bladed knife or cake tester comes out clean, about 1 hour. Let the cake cool in the pan for 5 to 10 minutes. Unmold the cake onto a deep plate to catch the juices and let it cool to room temperature before cutting. Pry off any pineapple that may stick to the bottom of the pan and replace it onto the cake.

Serves 8

sweet anise custard

2½ cups soy milk

3 large star anise pods

1 tablespoon vanilla extract

1 cup sugar, divided

2 tablespoons apple cider vinegar

1½ tablespoons ginger juice
(see page 22)

1 teaspoon toasted sesame oil

½ teaspoon soy sauce

Red pepper flakes

Freshly ground white pepper

5 large eggs

I have wanted to create a Chinese version of baked custard for a long time. Recently, while reading a food magazine, it struck me: soy milk, of course. It acts in baking as milk does, so it is easy to substitute in recipes. Plus there are so many brands of soy milk available now and they taste better and better. I developed this custard originally with my chinablue Sweet Anise Glaze as the topping. The recipe below is a variation that may at first seem odd because of the spicing, but it is delicious.

Preheat the oven to 325° F. Bring a teakettle of water to a boil and keep it over low heat.

Heat the milk and star anise pods in a medium saucepan over low heat. Bring just to a boil, remove from the heat, add the vanilla, and let it stand for 15 minutes.

Meanwhile, heat ½ cup of the sugar with the vinegar in a small saucepan over medium-low heat. Stir until the sugar dissolves and the mixture comes to a simmer. Cook gently for several minutes. Add the ginger juice, oil, soy sauce, a tiny pinch of red pepper flakes, and a tiny pinch of white pepper and stir. Return the mixture to a simmer until it is syrupy, about 5 minutes. Immediately divide the sauce among four 1-cup ramekins. Tilt the molds to coat the bottoms and a bit of the sides evenly with the sauce. Set the prepared molds in a baking dish and set aside.

Whisk together the eggs and the remaining ½ cup sugar in a large bowl until smooth. While whisking, pour in the warm milk. Strain the mixture through a fine-mesh sieve into a large measuring cup or pitcher. Fill the prepared molds with the egg mixture and place the baking dish in the preheated oven. Pour enough hot water into the dish around the ramekins to come halfway up the sides of the molds. Bake until the custards are just set and a knife inserted in the center comes out clean, about 1 hour.

Transfer the custards to a rack to cool to room temperature, and then refrigerate them until cold, at least 4 hours or overnight. To serve, run a knife around the edge of each and unmold onto a deep dessert plate.

Serves 4

strawberry-lemon tapioca

In Shanghai, desserts were made from scratch. A favorite of mine was an incredibly silky tapioca that we ate with fresh fruit. It was also incredibly time consuming to prepare. First, we made our own soy milk. We soaked the beans, ground them, squeezed out the milk, and then added tapioca, rock sugar (we didn't use granulated), and strands of natural gelatin to help it set. In Chinatown, tapioca is usually made with more eggs so it is more yellow, a lucky color for Chinese. Yellow symbolizes wealth and prosperity.

Lemon Sauce

1 teaspoon cornstarch

⅓ cup freshly squeezed lemon juice

¼ cup sugar

2 tablespoons honey

Salt

Tapioca

2¾ cups whole milk

⅓ cup sugar

3 tablespoons instant tapioca

1 large egg

½ teaspoon cinnamon

1 teaspoon vanilla extract

1 pint ripe strawberries, hulled

1½ teaspoons sugar, divided

2 tablespoons sliced almonds

To make the lemon sauce: Stir the cornstarch together with a little of the lemon juice in a small bowl and set aside. Measure the remaining lemon juice, sugar, honey, and a pinch of salt into a small pan and bring them to a simmer over medium-low heat. Stir the cornstarch mixture again, and then stir it into the pan. Cook gently, while stirring, for another minute. Remove the sauce from the heat, pour it into a bowl, and chill until needed.

To make the tapioca: Whisk together the milk, sugar, tapioca, egg, and cinnamon in a medium saucepan. Let the mixture stand for several minutes. Put the pan over medium heat and cook, stirring constantly, until the mixture comes to a boil. Remove from the heat, pour into a bowl, and stir in the vanilla. Chill until set.

continued

Put the strawberries in a medium bowl and sprinkle them lightly with about 1 teaspoon of the sugar. Refrigerate or let stand at room temperature for about 30 minutes.

Heat a small skillet over medium heat and add the almonds. Working quickly, dust the nuts with the remaining ½ teaspoon sugar. Toss and stir and, as soon as the nuts begin to brown, pour them onto a plate. Reserve.

Once the tapioca has firmed, divide it among dessert bowls. Stand the berries on top of the pudding and drizzle a spoonful of the lemon sauce over each. Scatter some of the almonds over each dessert and serve.

Serves 6 to 8

index

table of equivalents

The exact equivalents in the following tables have been rounded for convenience.

U.S.	METRIC
¼ teaspoon	1.25 milliliters
½ teaspoon	2.5 milliliters
1 teaspoon	5 milliliters
1 tablespoon (3 teaspoons)	15 milliliters
1 fluid ounce (2 tablespoons)	30 milliliters
¼ cup	60 milliliters
⅓ cup	80 milliliters
½ cup	120 milliliters
1 cup	240 milliliters
1 pint (2 cups)	480 milliliters
1 quart (4 cups, 32 ounces)	960 milliliters
1 gallon (4 quarts)	3.84 liters
1 ounce (by weight)	28 grams
1 pound	454 grams
2.2 pounds	1 kilogram

oven temperature

FAHRENHEIT	CELSIUS	GAS
250	120	½
275	140	1
300	150	2
325	160	3
350	180	4
375	190	5
400	200	6
425	220	7
450	230	8
475	240	9
500	260	10

length

U.S.	METRIC
⅛ inch	3 millimeters
¼ inch	6 millimeters
½ inch	12 millimeters
1 inch	2.5 centimeters